CODE BLUE IN THE WHITE HOUSE

WHAT SUCCESSFUL PRESIDENTS SELL VOTERS TO WIN ELECTIONS

CODE BLUE IN THE WHITE HOUSE

WHAT SUCCESSFUL PRESIDENTS SELL VOTERS TO WIN ELECTIONS

Jay Sordean, OMD, LAc

Bestselling Author and Speaker
As Seen on CBS, NBC, ABC, FOX, and CW

DEDICATION

This book is dedicated to all humans the world over, who have worked diligently for millennia to have the right to vote and representative governments.

May there be continued improvements in the election process -- to enable an even greater ability for voters in the United States to vote for the candidates they really believe in and trust, versus having to settle for the "lesser of two evils" as is often the feeling expressed by so many who vote or refuse to vote.

TABLE OF CONTENTS

Acknowledgments

Introduction: Presidential Politics in 2016

Chapter 1: WIFM: The station everyone listens to. Don't you?

Chapter 2: Successful Presidents: They Won and Why

Chapter 3: Getting Votes: Everything is Telling and Selling

Chapter 4: Human Psychology 101

Chapter 5: American Voter Psychology 101
- How are you related to "The Box?"
- Insider or Outsider
- Individuals vs Society
- "Us" versus "Them"
- Individual Responsibility versus Collective Cooperation
- Values versus Policy
- Addressing the Reptilian in Us All (The Survival Brain)
- Higher Brain Centers: Freedom, Individualism, Charity
- Winning and Competition
- Friends and Foes

Chapter 6. Archetypes to Understand Human Behavior and Then Speak to It
- General Discussion of Models of Psychology, Behavior, Values
- Specific models : DISC and B.A.N.K.
- Typing Past Presidents
- Typing Past Presidential Candidates

Chapter 7. Selling Techniques for the American Voter

Chapter 8: CODE BLUE or CODE RED in the White House? Current Presidential Candidates

Chapter 9: Research on Presidential Personality Typing

Chapter 10: Presidential Election Cycle Comedy

Chapter 11: Presidential Candidate Speeches & Books: What They Tell Us About Type and Selling.

Chapter 12: RESOURCES

Acknowledgments

All books and research involve numerous individuals and resources whose input, encouragement, editorial suggestions and inspiration are both critical and superfluous. To all of those below, both named and anonymous. I express my sincere thanks.

Let me also specifically thank the following:

-My family members, confidants, & politicians -- Savyon Sordean, Elah Sordean, Sigal Gafni, Erelah Gafni, Layla Gafni Kubukeli, Andrea Mintzer, Judy Sordean, Eliot Mintzer, Simone Coulars, Isa Coulars, Paul Weinberger, Hartmut Gerdes, Lynda Griffith, Marijke Coulars, Koji Onitsuka, Anthony Freeman, Dr. Byron Fong, Jeremy Smith, Simon Gibson, Mayors Tom Bates, Loni Hancock, and Takeyama (Sakai, Japan), Juri and Linda Komendant, Ronald V. Dellums, Ying Lee Kelly, Nancy Skinner, Mayor Lugar, Jerry Brown

Those who were early supporters in purchasing the Kindle edition of Code Blue, making this book a number one bestseller. Authors w,ho have written books on politics, sales, personality typing, psychology, physiology, philosophy.

Cheri Tree, Jenny Luetkemeyer, Esther Wildenberg, Anna Parker and Marc Gleeman at BANKCODE.

My colleagues and coauthors around the world, in PnP, and Magic Messengers, Clint Arthur and Alison Savitch.

Co-participants at B.A.N.K.™ Code Training Programs, patients at The Redwood Clinic, Health Clinic attendees at John F. Kennedy University, various folks and friends in Japan, and all others who participated in personality coding surveys related to the presidents.

And last, all of the past presidents, past losing presidential candidates, current presidential candidates, political parties, the United States' political system, spin-meisters, speech writers, future presidential hopefuls, TV and written media outlets, comedians on TV and stage, and the American Voter or Non-Voter -- who are the reason why this subject exists in the first place.

Introduction: Presidential Politics in 2016

Bill Clinton was a palm-presser. George W. Bush was a partying frat-boy. Jimmy Carter was a peanut farmer who builds houses for the poor. Ronald Reagan was a movie star in early stages of Alzheimer's. George H.W. Bush was the head of the CIA with long ties with the Kings of Saudi Arabia. Richard Nixon was a Quaker.

Wait just a minute. You are telling me that Richard Nixon was a Quaker???!!!

All successful presidential candidates who became the President of the United States of America have a story. Each has had a style unique unto themselves. And they all had to sell themselves to the voters to win.

Values versus Policy. Emotions versus Logic. Us versus Them. These and other dichotomies are concepts that presidential candidates use in their speeches and body language. Selling these to the voters can win elections.

This year, 2016, is a big election year in the United States. For the past year, various candidates have "hit the campaign trail" with a goal of becoming President of the United States. The President of the United States is arguably one of the most (if not THE most) powerful positions in the world. Of course, there are other government positions up for selection as well, but the presidential contest always creates more buzz and excitement every 4 years than almost any other national political campaign.

Almost invariably, the President comes from either the Democratic or the Republican political parties. So while the other parties have their candidates vying to win in November, the Democratic and Republican parties each have had numerous candidates wanting to get their party's endorsement. What has been unusual this time (2015-2016) around is the introduction of a "maverick" Republican candidate who did not come out of the political ranks of career politicians.

Donald J. Trump is not the only non-politician who has decided to run for President. Other business executives like Ross Perot and Carly Fiorina have put forth valiant efforts in the past, but no other business executive really came close to getting the party nomination. Why they were unsuccessful will be touched upon later.

On the other hand, just getting a party nomination does not assure that the candidate will be elected to the Presidency. There are lots of hurdles to cross to become President of the United States of America. And sometimes it involves selection by the Supreme Court. So you don't really have to even be elected, but you do have to get close enough in the general election to have a Supreme Court decision put you into the Oval Office.

Regardless, getting to the party convention and being chosen by the Republican or Democratic parties as their candidate does require some ability to convince enough people to vote for you, whether in a primary, at a caucus, at the

Congressional level, at the national party-boss level, or at the party convention.

Regardless, getting to the party convention and being chosen by the Republican or Democratic parties as their candidate does require some ability to convince enough people to vote for you, whether in a primary, at a caucus, at the Congressional level, at the national party-boss level, or at the party convention.

What are the ways that these people communicate so that people (#1) pay attention to them and (#2) vote for them? Just how do these candidates convince voters to care? And do they have the ability to convince enough voters to elect them in November? I hope to explore that from the perspective of what I think is needed, and what historically has been used, to sell the voters. In other words, exactly what is needed to predict the behavior and values of the electorate and use that to effectively sell them on a new President.

Chapter 1: WIFM: The station everyone listens to, don't you?

Call me old-fashioned or call me cynical. Either way for those who know what a radio is, and even for those modern techies who haven't heard of or seen a radio, EVERYONE listens to the radio station with the call letters WIFM.

"W" "I" "F" "M"

Now you might be thinking, "W.I.F.M.? I don't listen to that. I have never even heard of it."

Shortly, you will see that in fact you do listen to that station even if you don't remember. In fact, not only do you listen to it but you identify with it and groove along with it more often than you think. So sorry, you have forgotten or just not been aware of it. WIFM

We will get back to that shortly, but now for a little background.

For those who do not know, the call letters for radio (and television) stations in the United States are all 4 letters long. They also have a frequency number that they are associated with. This is whether you are listening on the AM or the FM dials. On the west coast, like in California where I live, the stations are named

KFOG, KQED, KJAZ, etc. On the east coast they are WALW, WISH, WXZZ, etc. WISH is a station in Indianapolis which I know of because I grew up in Indianapolis, so of course I remember that call sign.

So, in short, the ones east of the Mississippi start with a "W" and the ones west of the Mississippi start with a "K." So maybe you have never been east of the Mississippi so you didn't know that there was a "WIFM" (even though you listen to it! I insist).

So, <u>what about</u> this radio station WIFM that I talk of, claiming that it is the radio station we all listen to? Well, I first heard about this radio station at a business networking group I used to be a part of many years ago. And the pronouncement that everyone listens to it was made by Gary Buffon.

Each of us other networking members was looking at each other and were saying "I don't listen to that, do you?" Just like you are saying to yourself as well right now. But hear me out and you might change your mind. You might find that you do listen to WIFM.

What's In It For Me. Let me repeat that. What's In it For Me . W.I.F. M. Now do you think that you listen to it?

Now this may be a little cynical, as I said previously, but I think it is quite true, because of our make-up as humans. There are many, many times we are trying to figure out and decide "If I do this, or I do that", or "If I buy this or if I buy that" we think "what's in it for me." at a fundamental survival level. Although perhaps we are unaware of it because it happens at such an unconscious level in our brain.

I think you will agree that we don't buy food because we don't like how it tastes. We don't buy food for purely altruistic purposes. Even when we buy or acquire food for others, for the greater good, there is still the thought "what tastes good to me?" Or, "this would taste good for my family." The collective "we" still includes "me" by definition.

Or maybe we also buy something as a gift for someone else. We are thinking (actually talking to our self, inside our head) "Maybe this would make a good gift for...." We think of the other person in choosing it, but somewhere deep inside we want the other person to enjoy it and we get some satisfaction from that as well. We feel good about thinking about someone else we are giving the gift to. Even though we are thinking about others, there is still at least a little WIFM in the gift giving, and thus in everything we do.

So, when we realize and accept the premise that we humans all listen to WIFM at least part of the day, it is logical to say that politicians, who want to sell themselves to us, have to know this concept as well.

The politicians and candidates will try to figure out how to address the self-serving interests of the voter. "Self-serving interest" being the focus of WIFM.

Voters listen to programs other than WIFM. Politicians also have to know what other stations the voters listen to so they can craft their message to speak to those issues also.

Many radio stations have a predominant theme. Talk radio is particularly powerful and targeted. The talk radio show host is talking to the listener, just like the person is talking to themselves in their own head.

People often like to listen to opinions similar to their own. There are also a few people who like to listen to other viewpoints just to challenge their own assumptions or for intellectual stimulation. But mostly people want to listen to people saying what they already believe.

So what are some of the talk radio show themes?

-Religious talk radio

-Conservative talk radio

-Liberal talk radio

-Left wing talk radio

-Social justice talk radio

-Local city council talk radio

-Cultural talk radio

-Car-talk

-Etc.

Now, it is true that politicians, being like all other human beings in certain ways, also listen to WIFM. So, if you are a voter, perhaps you will want to consider the question "How MUCH does the candidate / politician listen to WIFM?" In other words, how self-serving is this candidate, how much are they just thinking about what they can get out of running for office, and how much are they doing it for service, for the "honor" of being a "public servant?"

Is the presidential candidate saying, in words, actions, and history, "It's all about ME, ME, ME!!!" Are they all about image? Are they all about themselves or about the team?

People hear a lot of lip service about people wanting a
government-paid or government-salaried job
because they want to go into "public service." It often has
more to do with hoping to get a lifetime job with a pension
plan (that really don't exist in any private industry much
anymore) than it does with actually serving the public. Don't
get me wrong. There are those in government jobs who do try
to do good for the people who are paying their salary. But
when it comes to career politicians, or business-person-
turned-politician, I have to think that they are there to get
whatever they can get out of it.

What can they get out of it, you are pondering (I hope)? By
being President of the United States of America, besides riding
around in Air Force One? Besides the upper 0.5% of the
population salary, guaranteed for life, full medical insurance
benefits for life, body-guards for life, and ready-made, instant-
demand set-up for million dollar speeches?

Like lots of power. Like lots of new connections with important people all around the world who wouldn't give them the time of day just as a business person. Being President of the United States? Now that is a phone call most people would pick up on or at least return if they got a phone message.

So, in summary, VOTERS need to know about WIFM and figure out where the candidates stand on this.

If you are voting to improve your own life, or the life of your family members, or of your community, city, state, country, or even of the world, you HAVE to make this assessment. Because, if for no other reason, the presidential candidates are for sure trying to be the WIFM station you are listening to. Because everyone is listening to WIFM every day.

We will be talking a bit more about this WIFM concept later when we are talking about personality types and talking about speech writers for politicians and the politicians themselves.

Chapter 2: Successful Presidents: They Won and Why

Styles of the Successful Presidents

All of the former, and current Presidents are successful by definition. They got elected. They successfully got elected in one way or another. Each President has had different personalities and personal backgrounds. All of the presidents since Eisenhower and the 1950's came out of politics -- as Senators, Governors, Vice Presidents, etc. Some of the presidents won on their first attempt. Others had to run a couple of times.

Each president has had a particular style that they were known for. It could have been a stiffness or a "good ol' boy" attitude. They might have been more intellectual or maybe they mostly saw it as an opportunity to vacation often and have others steer and run "the ship."

None of them received 100% of the electorate (Electoral College) or popular vote. See chart below.

The entire American electorate never votes at every election. In more recent presidential elections around a maximum of 60% of the eligible voters had their ballots counted. The Presidents only have to win enough of the popular vote to get the Electoral College vote as a majority. If one is counting the popular votes, we might actually see that "none of the above/not voted" actually would win every time if the non-voters' non-vote had also been counted. George W. Bush won without winning the popular vote in Y2K. In 1992, 1996, and 2000 the winner did not even garner 50% of the popular vote. In each of those years third party candidates got part of the popular vote, although none of those 3rd party candidates got any Electoral College votes.

Examples of the Electoral College / popular vote counts for presidential races are as follows:

Year	Winner	EC Votes	Loser	% Popular vote
2012	Obama/Biden	332/205	Romney/Paul	57.1% / 47.2%
2008	Obama/Biden	365/173	McCain/Palin	52.9% / 45.7%
2004	Bush/Cheney	286/251	Kerry/Edwards	50.7% / 48.3%

2000 Bush/Cheney   271/266 Gore/Lieberman 47.9% / 48.4%

Nader/LaDuke   2.7%

1996 Clinton/Gore   379/159 Dole/Kemp   49.2% / 40.7%

Perot/Choate   8.4%

1992 Clinton/Gore   370/168 Bush/Quayle   43.0% / 37.4%

Perot/Stockdale 18.9%

1988 Bush/Quayle 426/111 Dukakis/Bentson 53.4% / 45.6%

1984 Reagan/Bush 525/13   Mondale/Ferraro 58.8% / 40.6%

1980 Reagan/Bush 489/49   Carter/Mondale   50.7% / 41.0%

Anderson/Lucey   6.6%

(Source: http://www.presidency.ucsb.edu/showelection.php?year=_____)

All of that mathematical technicality aside, let's look at some of the personality styles of the Presidents that might have helped them to win the elections.   Note that this is by no means and exhaustive expose or analysis of these particular Presidents. It is just a snapshot of selected impressions by myself and others who should know.

Presidential Personality Styles

BILL CLINTON. Palm pressing: According to John Corcoran, who worked in the Clinton White House, "Bill Clinton was known for spending more time on a rope line than most politicians. I was at events where the speeches would wrap up and he would spend another 45 minutes to an hour working his way up and down the rope line, shaking hands, taking pictures, and having brief conversations.

In fact, he was incredible at networking with people at face-to-face events. That's where he really shined.

His attitude was if people came out to hear him, often waiting for hours just for a glimpse of the President, then he would try hard to make sure everyone had an opportunity to shake his hand, get a quick picture, or just wave hello.

You don't have to be President to implement this strategy. It's about giving the gift of your time to others."

Was there also any business acumen that Bill Clinton brought to the table? Had he created successful businesses or businesses that had failed or caused him to declare bankruptcy? I don't recall Bill Clinton campaigning on his career in business. So being a businessman is not necessarily an asset to winning the White House.

GEORGE W. BUSH was known as a frat boy, a partier, as a person who gave a nickname to everyone he met, including high officials from other countries. It was this "familiarity" that he promoted with those around him as well as to the voting population that seemed to make him a "man of the people." Of course, he also had Karl Rove in his entourage creating political mischief to help improve his chances. But this "good ol' boy" persona, this "familiarity," seemed to make many people able to identify with him, to make him feel close to them. It was what got him sufficient votes in the primary and the general elections to be able to have his presidency decided by the Supreme Court.

There is also the famous (and controversial) video of President Bush reading a story to children at the time of the plane crashes into the World Trade Center Towers in New York City. Video footage and timelines of the day showed that he continued to finish reading for some number of minutes after being informed. Does this suggest that his deep humanity led him to continue to read? Was he afraid of hurting the young students' feelings by having to get up and leave suddenly? Was this part of the personhood of President Bush that people saw before the election and moved them to vote for him?

Various magazine articles chronicled "W"s business ventures prior to election. And it didn't matter that many of his significant businesses were failures or paid for by Saudi Arabian investors. Many were said to want access to his father, George H. W. Bush, President at the time "W" was trying to find his own way in life. So perhaps again, being in business, and failing repeatedly in those ventures even with the help of OPM, doesn't seem to be a key determining factor in winning the presidency.

JIMMY CARTER was a man of the people. While he had a successful peanut farm prior to entering the White House, his Southern Charm and warmth helped people feel like they could relate to him. According to interviews President Carter gave on national public radio, after his presidency, he returned to a farm that was deeply in the red. He and Rosalyn almost divorced because the strain of bankruptcy and being together so much time AFTER the presidency. As he said in his radio interview I happened to listen to, he and Rosalyn figured out a way to have their own lives and interact enough during the day to continue to like each other and stay married.

But it was Jimmy Carter's ability to talk in front of the American public about such personal details of his life, showing his vulnerability, which made him so relatable to common people. At least I personally felt like he was concerned about the welfare of and cared about the "common person."

Also, as a major proponent and participant in Habitat for Humanity, Jimmy Carter enlisted the community in helping others rebuild homes. He really showed his caring for other people, the community, church life, and charitable activities.

Jimmy Carter happened to have a background in business, successful, then failing, then again successful. Business acumen is likely something people didn't know about candidate Carter prior to the election. I certainly didn't until his open and honest interview on national public radio.

President Carter also installed solar panels on the White House roof during his presidency. They remained there until Ronald Reagan won and had the removed.

BARACK OBAMA showed his humanity by working early on in his career in community organizing in Chicago before he became Senator and then President. Apparently, this was after he graduated from Harvard School of Law and was the editor of the Law Review, a prestigious position. Many wondered why he would give up a lucrative law career and go back to work in communities.

As the one of the college athletes who has been in the White House, his ability to stand tall (many presidents have been above average height, an advantage in winning elections due to primitive beliefs we humans have hard wired in our brains) and speak with eloquence has served him well and may have been a factor in his winning the election.

There was also the fact that he was running against John McCain and Sarah Palin.

I personally think and feel that President Obama is a decent man and a great representative of the U.S. while I have some issues with some of his policies and actions. That aside, his ability to shed authentic tears of sadness giving speeches about the mass murders of children, theatre goers, LGBT partiers and others should give most people a respect for a man who deeply cares about other people.

Business and Mr. Obama? I don't know anything about his business ventures or success.

RONALD REAGAN: "Ronnie" was a famous Hollywood actor and ex-governor of California before winning the presidency. He was considered to be conservative and have a warm smile and handshake. Some called him the "Great Communicator." He cut federal income taxes for the rich and dramatically increased the U.S. military budget. In California he is credited with emptying the mental hospitals, therefore increasing the homelessness of the mentally ill. On the other hand, it is said that his massive U.S. military buildup helped, perhaps, to bankrupt the Soviet Union trying to compete with the U.S. militarily.

The Berlin wall came down during his administration largely due to the policies and actions of Mikhail Gorbachev whom he developed a personal connection with. The Iran Contra Affair also occurred during his tenure. Ronald Reagan is remembered very fondly by most Republicans and is hailed as an icon and model to emulate.

Summary of Success

So, in looking at all of the above Presidents, what helped their success in winning? All had to be leaders, and all had to show their humanity to get elected. Their business acumen, or lack of success therein, was not a key factor in their electability, apparently. Political connections? Ivy League or other elite college's connections? Definitely the latter two for many of the ones mentioned.

At the Heights of the Presidency: Does Tall Matter?

Psychologists and anthropologists have found that tall does
matter from a biological standpoint. The dominant males of
the species often command the tribe. That applies to many
species. It also applies to humans, and not only in the U.S.

It was pointed out that Saddam Hussein was a tall man (6' 1",
186 cm). He was ruthless but his height was no doubt a
commanding power that psychologically had its effects in
Iraq. This is just one example of foreign leaders whose height
made a difference. In the past before the advent of television
which can distort anything (:)), the physical presence of a
candidate or President (or General for that matter) made a
difference as far as their first impression power of selling.

At the opposite side of the spectrum, we have only to think
about the "Napoleon complex" spoken about so much, to see
how influential this may be unconsciously, even if we want to
think that we educated humans are intellectually above and
uninfluenced by size. Just think about the survival brain.
Would you rather face a mouse or a polar bear? Which
commands more respect?

We are not talking about athletes here, but they also illustrate the point well. Very tall and large basketball players draw the attention of the crowd. Large football and soccer players draw the attention of the crowd. Athletes don't have to be large to dominate in a field--however in certain sports they certainly have an advantage over shorter players, even in swimming, as Michael Phelps demonstrates.

Again, you can't just be taller to win in sports. You have to be great at it. You have to practice and train. You have to psychologically prepare to be ridiculed. But, the psychological advantage of being tall is there, in spite of the myths of David and Goliath and others.

So here is the run down on heights of the US President's according to internet and Wikipedia investigations.

6' 4"	1.93 m	Abraham Lincoln
6' 3.5"	1.92 m	Lyndon Baines Johnson (LBJ)
6' 2"	1.88 m	Bill Clinton
6' 2"	1.88 m	George HW Bush
6' 1'	1.86 m	Barack Obama
6' 1"	1.86 m	Ronald Reagan

6' 0"	1.84 m	John F. Kennedy (JFK)
5' 11.5"	1.83 m	Richard Nixon
5' 11.5"	1.83 m	George W Bush
5' 9.5"	1.77 m	Jimmy Carter

The heights of a variety of other political figure, famous people and comedians can be found in the resources chapter at the end of this book.

Of course, there is absolutely no correlation between size and intelligence. But, taller men and women command, and often get, more attention than shorter people, throughout their lives, especially when they are standing side by side with someone less tall. Perhaps this is one reason for the media attention that the 6' 3" Donald Trump garners? And how will Hillary Rodham Clinton fare at 5' 4.5" (164 cm).

Chapter 3: Getting Votes: Everything is Telling and Selling

Selling is Basic Human Nature

After all, becoming a political candidate and getting elected is about SELLING yourself.

> -- Selling who you are to campaign supporters,

> -- Selling who you are to campaign money contributors,

> -- Selling yourself to voter registration advocates,

> -- Selling yourself to other candidates who will support you,

> -- and (perhaps) especially, selling yourself to the voter.

What can you say or be that will motivate someone to take the time to go vote and also vote for you?

Some people think "selling" is somehow lower level behavior. That it is nasty, bad, something that makes them feel uncomfortable. Many people say "I cannot sell." or "I hate selling." "It is known that great sales people are rare but get paid lots of money."

Others have clearly pointed out the fallacy of thinking that selling is base or bad, stating that "EVERYTHING IS SELLING."

So, where do you stand on this debate? Is selling good or bad? Or is it just the product being sold that is good or bad or neutral, not the act of selling, itself.

I fall on the side of thinking "everything is selling." The argument that convinced me is the observation that even in the day-to-day interactions I have with loved ones, "selling" is involved frequently.

When we are trying to get our children up and out of the door for school and they are dawdling, we have to convince them to get going. The act of "convincing" is a form of "selling."

All parents, teachers, siblings, grandparents, and others who get the joy of being with young children know that there is a science and an art to selling the child on what you'd like or need them to do. Like, maybe they won't eat something that is great for them. Or, maybe you are all going somewhere and they are not cooperating. Or you need to get some sleep and they won't go to sleep. All of these situations require some form of selling or convincing.

Parents and grandparents, aunts and uncles, baby sitters, nannies, and caregivers, you ALL know what I'm talking about.

In the best of situations verbal communication will do the trick. If we know the "tricks" needed to convince the child. Speaking nicely, cajoling, persuading – or threatening removal of rewards, giving "time-out" like consequences – either the "carrot" or "the stick" approaches. Using "reverse psychology."

While largely discredited now as psychologically and physically unhealthy for children, the "paddle on the rear end" technique was popular in the 50's white suburbia when I was growing up. Thank you to Dr. Spock. It is still seen in many families and the use of a hand or fist in "delivering the message" is "the stick" approach, literally. This method of "selling" is not something I recommend as it is coercion or forced behavioral modification. The bottom line is that some form of selling is basic human behavior and we all can learn to sell others in more effective and less violent ways. In fact, we must learn more effective and less coercive ways to sell and knowing how people behave is the most clever way to go about it.

Even Rich Politicians Learn to Sell

It is common sense that the most persuasive political candidates know how to sell. They study it. And the business-oriented candidates also got where they are by selling themselves to others. When the candidate starts out in a family with lots of money, like Donald Trump, George W. Bush, George H.W.Bush, etc., they don't have the same pressure to learn to sell themselves intrinsically for survival purposes.

Compare the life they start out in to that of children who have to sift through trash piles every day to find something to help fill their stomachs. The person who "won the sperm lottery" or "genetic roulette" and was born into riches probably has never even trash picked. My point being that the deepest levels of starvation and destitution push the survival drive -- you have no choice but to learn to sell yourself to survive. No one else is there with bounty to make it easy. Think of the movie "Slum Dog Millionaire" for a Bollywood spin on the concept.

However, even those born with a "silver spoon in their mouth" still learn how to sell themselves to their parents, siblings, and to the rest of the relevant world. It is not from the same deeply-rooted, daily near-death experiences of the impoverished, but it still is a level of learning to survive in the circumstances one is born into.

"What might these "tumultuous and trying" circumstances the uber wealthy have to endure?" the less-well-off of us readers might be wondering in total disbelief. Well, it could be like a very money-conscious and tight-fisted parental attitude displayed by some of the early Rockefeller matriarchs. Dolling out small allowances and having every child using hand-me-down clothes to appreciate what they have (or at least this was the theme in one movie I watched about that family.) It could be growing up in a large family and having to maneuver the usual dynamics of sibling alliances and sibling rivalries.

Of course, you only-child readers might not be able to personally relate to this, but your friends will surely enlighten you on their struggles along the way. Or, it could be a rich parent who resents the attention that his or her spouse showers on the child, and thus makes it hard on the child to flourish.

I could go on and on with other speculative examples about how both the rich and the poor child have to learn to sell to survive. Whatever the situation, we ALL, rich and poor, have to learn to sell ourselves to survive and flourish in our families, community, and economic world.

The Currency of Politicians: Sales Acumen

Politicians in particular though have sales acumen as their currency. If they can't sell, they can't run for office.

The sales may be fund-raising abilities, creating teams of people who will volunteer for them, or of captivating the imagination of the party machinery. But, they always have to be selling to survive in politics.

And they can't do it alone. Besides the tens of millions it costs at minimum, they have to create a sales team and sales department around them. That is the campaign and it includes the foot soldiers who call on phones and walk door to door. Like the old time door-to-door encyclopedia, Fuller Brush, or vacuum cleaner sellers.

My grandfather Wow-Wow (his nickname) told me stories of his sales experiences when selling Electrolux vacuum cleaners door-to-door. One time he went into a home and proceeded to pull up the bed sheets and vacuumed the area at the "foot" of the bed, the place where people's feet go to rest when sleeping. After vacuuming the foot of the bed, he then opened the machine, took out the vacuum bag, and poured out the contents back onto the sheet. It was a pile of dirt. Needless to say, either the ensuing disgust or the embarrassment led to a handsome sale for him. Politicians are the same.

You do what you have to do to make the sale, so politicians either sell the voters on themselves or they try to sell someone on the idea of throwing the election – thus winning by the use of fraud. Maybe they do it by slinging mud at the other person, or they show how clean they can make the world of the future.

What about the "Telling" in this chapter title "Telling and Selling" you ask? "Telling" is all the words that politicians use to convince others of the buying proposition that "I am the one you should support and vote for." While each of us in some fashion and in many daily situations is telling and selling others, politicians just play on a bigger stage. And perhaps they also are more calculating in their understanding of human psychology and voter psychology.

These are our next topics.

Chapter 4: Human Psychology 101

As more fully discussed in <u>Super Brain: Maximize Your Brain Health for a Better Life,</u> we humans have a nervous system that is first of all designed for survival and propagation of the species. Thus, we have structures that are designed for physical preservation and then structures that are designed for higher level surviving, thriving, and spiritual development. At each level of neural organization there are increasing abilities to synthesize information, integrate experiences, and suppress the most basic of emotions and feelings of hunger, sexual desire, and fear reactions. These brain stem and reptilian areas of the brain are deep in the central nervous system, work automatically in many respects, and are the first order of filtering of external stimulation and input.

Thus, what you see, hear, taste, smell, and feel all initially go through the survival brain and we have at least an unconscious reaction to them before our higher powers can kick in. This process is very very fast, in fractions of a second.

So fast as to be imperceptible. When we hear a speech that speaks of something scary we perk up and become alert. Because our survival and that of our family and progeny may be at stake. Or the survival of our tribe.

This issue of fear as a primary focus of the survival brain is fascinating to the higher parts of your brain. Theories state that we actually reward ourselves for noticing fear reactions: we have areas of our brain that are the "trophy room of negatives." This trophy room can become so full and so dominant that we can forgo positives for the comfort of acquiring more fear-based trophies of negative consequences.

While that may not make much sense to you the way I described it, the bottom line is that when we are prompted by outside stimuli to have a fear reaction, we wake up and take note of the importance of the next things presented to us. It is like we smelled a bear coming into our cave and we then prepared to run out of the cave or stay and fight. The bear then becomes the object of fear and dread. (Of course, this presupposes that we are not living in a state of harmonious communication with this theoretical bear-- and the threat becomes a theoretical non-threat or welcome response. Think Smokey the Bear(™).)

So when a politician evokes a fear response in a very deliberate way, by saying certain words in certain ways to us, after we have this unconscious survival fear response, the next words can unconsciously become the objects of dread and negativity. It is a very simple and well known pattern. Master manipulators and even naive summer camp campfire story tellers know how to do this in a scary nighttime story. This response has been studied extensively by scientists and the masters of sales. It is even well known to those who want to go beyond selling ethically and trick us into buying something or some idea that is untrue and against our own better judgment. Of course, politicians and Presidents would <u>never</u> do that to the American public.

Then again, it is fact that Secretary of State Colin Powell convinced the United Nations that Saddam Hussein has weapons of mass destruction. He and the Bush administration also told and sold the American public on that notion, In fact, there were no weapons of mass destruction and there were many in the White House who knew that. But this illustrates how politicians do use fear to change perception right after they use fear to trick the brain into thinking the next words were true and something to fear.

Negativity and "No"

At least in the English-speaking world, the use of the word "No" is thought to be one of the most widely used words to communicate to children about what to do or not do. Parents and guardians want to at least protect the infant, toddler, and child who may be vulnerable to a new food, non-food, traffic situation, playground hazard, etc. Learning NOT to do or

where NOT to go is necessary for us all to learn and survive.

These are examples of why the word "No" is ingrained into our brains so deeply and so often. Thus, to get the attention of a voter, using the word "No" in adequate numbers of times in a speech will be hitting on that deep spot, including an unconscious association of that word with an authority figure who you should pay attention to in order to enhance your personal safety.

These are just a couple of the deep psychological processes going on in our brains that makes our response to candidates messages more likely to have us favor or not favor a particular candidate.

And they know it.

In short, in our personal development from age 0 to 120, we go from surviving to thriving (hopefully). We begin very dependent, then move to more independence, leading to responsibility and replication. But the survival need and psychology is still there, ever cautious.

Chapter 5: American Voter 101

Our human brain has higher levels of functioning than the survival brain. The neocortex exemplifies this higher level of operation. There are various ways that our brain has categorized information. Those categories tell us things like who to trust, who to avoid, what to choose, what to reject, and millions of other judgments and interpretations.

In this chapter I am going to go over some of the more key concepts and opposites that play into the decision-making process of the voter in choosing who to vote for. Part of these are related to our tribal orientation as humans. Part of these are related to our sense of safety or our willingness to take risk. And still others are related to rights of the individual in conjunction with obligations of the collective.

The "above survival" aspects of American voter psychology include freedom of speech, freedom of religion, rugged individualism, dreams of riches, freedom to go into any job you want and can get or create, helping others, supporting the family, winning, democracy, privacy and private property.

How are you related to "The Box" and
Where Do YOU Fit in "The Box"

Certain people act, and think, "within the box." They follow
rules and get upset when others don't follow the rules. People
in the military follow orders. People working on the job at a
fast-food store have particular rules and processes they follow
to make the food consistent day in and day out. Workers who
assemble computer components, formulate medications in a
pharmaceutical factory, and put together automobiles
(alongside the robots) all have a set of rules and steps they
follow to create the right product that can be replicated. This
mind set and behavior is called the BLUEPRINT type in the
B.A.N.K.™ CODE system and most likely the "C" in the DISC
system.

By necessity and circumstance, we all need to work within the
box in various situations. Without it, societies would not
function very efficiently. In fact, without it there would be no
society. Bus, train, and air schedules would be way off. There
are steps that have to be taken for a law to be passed by
Congress. There are steps that are supposed to be taken

before soldiers are sent off to fight. There are steps involved in choosing and electing a president. Following the rules helps prevent chaos and creates greater predictability. On the other hand, it can also stifle innovation. Nevertheless, it is important that at least part of the population be working within the box all the time, and everyone else working within the box at least part of the time.

Other people are considered to be operating "outside the box." Donald Trump even wrote a book about being outside the box. Bernie Sanders is also not your mainstream politician in his philosophy and stances. Both might be considered to be operating outside the box.

The irony comes in to play by realizing that once you are elected President you are firmly inside a predetermined role that has certain roles and protocols you are expected to follow. That position is controlled by a 200 plus year old tradition that is being inside the box, as a "BLUEPRINT" (B-type role). You become a "Code Blue in the White House."

Insider or Outsider: Inside the Beltway (DC) / Outside Political Arenas

Politicians love to have a "me versus them" object. Who can they point to to distinguish themselves from? Who can I point to as the bad or incompetent one so that I am by comparison great and competent? For people who are in or work with the federal government, their lingo includes the term "inside the beltway." What does that mean?

In essence, this means the federal government, White House, Congress, Departments and agencies. Because they are located inside the highway, the Beltway that goes around Washington, DC. The District of Columbia. An area of land that is the land of the US government.

People who work inside the beltway are the ones who make the federal laws and enforce or carry them out. (Of course, there are other large agencies, like the CIA and the Pentagon which are outside the beltway).

So, anytime there is "gridlock" in Congress, when the two major parties can't agree on something, or on anything, and it seems that there are problems resulting from that, even the politicians who are part of the gridlock will claim to be "outside" the beltway -- that way the troublemakers, the no-gooders, the obstructionists, the "them" are the other people inside the beltway. This insider / outsider dichotomy, gambit, is played by many current candidates (like Governors) and particularly by Donald Trump, who has never worked as a government employee inside the beltway.

Some voters hate the federal government so much that anyone "outside the Beltway" already has instant credibility.

And given that the creation of the United States of America is based on a rebellion against another government and taxation (actually it was corporate favoritism in tax structure, not simply taxation), this antipathy to the federal government is somewhat ingrained in what it means to be an American. Thus, by design, insiders to the Beltway area at least a little bit suspect by definition.

Immigrants vs Native Born

Modern America (more properly called the United States of America) is a nation of immigrants. Even the native Americans are immigrants from another continent according to anthropologists. Of course, though, the Native American tribes existed here long before the European explorers came to "discover" these lands and bring a new way to "steward" the land and animals through land ownership.

Waves of immigration from around the world are the legacy of this land mass. Sequestering Native American tribes into their own tracts of lands, and separate and semiautonomous states, is also a legacy. And along the way many people have been born to parents who were birthing while on this land mass. So, there is a mixture of immigrant and native born people living here together. It has always been that way for hundreds, if not thousands, of years.

People born on this land mass, the "native born," have a feeling of specialness. This is not unlike the feeling people born in other countries feel. One's "native village" is a deep-seated psychological construct of the brain that is intrinsic and thus very powerful.

Public and private and home-based education have an influence on this feeling in the individual. Sometimes it enhances it -- those people are very "patriotic" and feel a deep loyalty to the "native village," "home town," "state I was born and reared in," "my country 'tis of thee." Teaching the history of a country in standard school curriculum binds all people's in the country to a common feeling of ties and patriotism. On the other hand, recent immagrants and children of recent immigrants (but native born) may have very close cultural ties to the country of origin of the immigrants. These deep cultural ties, language, holidays, religious practices and beliefs, all can temper the feelings of "patriotism" for the new country. And they can also create a conflict in that new "native born" person's mind. Maybe they exist with a split cultural loyalty, or they never embrace the new cultural identity as an "American" and instead identify with their parents' homeland.

The past 40 years or more have also been a time when "discovering and respecting your roots" has been an important part of personal and family growth for many Americans.

And of course there is the question of what really is <u>authentic</u> "American" culture. Given the "melting pot" theme, imagine the difference between a pureed vegetable soup to a stew. American culture is more like a stew while French or German cultures are more like a pureed vegetable soup. (Although that homogeneity of culture has broken down in the past decades more and more.) The American "melting pot" stew is a soup with lots of still-clearly identifiable fully formed chunks of food mixed in with each other. The pieces of the stew, vegetables, spices, meat / tofu / veggie beef, whatever bump up against each other and create a culinary delight but each flavor is still identifiable and strong.

On the other stove burner, the pureed vegetable soup has all the components so blended that there is a predominant flavor and texture that is distinct. It is also a wonderful thing to imbibe and enjoy, but it is a different way to make an edible.

So, when politicians try to use this "immigrant versus 'native born'" concept as a political hot button, they will open up some deep psychological and cultural responses. For some of the more "patriotic - America for Americans" type of voters, this topic may spur them to attend rallies and speeches and give money. These voters may view things more in two choices, two contrasts. Black versus white, or black and white. Not 50 shades of gray.

However, for others, the issue is more complex. Using the immigration issue, legal or otherwise, to drum up personal support will only confuse them. For them, immigration is not a "black or white" issue, and mention of "building a wall" creates an opposite response or a confused thought. In sales, a confused thought is a person who will not buy. A "wall" means to some, "Vote YES." To others it means "I'm on the other side of the issue and don't want a wall between me and my dreams."

Nevertheless, immigration is a hot-button concept in human's psychology and is thus one tool in the politician's or candidate's tool box of building blocks to try to construct their vote getting machine.

Individuals vs Society: and Government

One key idea typically associated with Americanism is individualism. Standing on your own two feet. Being a "self-made man or woman." The stories of the precolonial era are rife with the explorers of the continent who were alone or in small teams, mapping out the "territory" and meeting the native tribes to learn more and trade goods.

This idea of going it alone is certainly based on some aspects of human psychology. We are born into this world usually alone (unless we are a twin, triplet, quadruplet, quintuplets, or…), in school we are having to memorize things into our own (individual) head, we move around as an individual being, we have an individual name (some cultures may not have this, but in American culture we have an individualizing name), we get a Social Security Number that is unique to each of us, we each have to put food and liquids down our own mouth to get nourishment, etc. etc.

So, biologically, psychologically, and culturally we have a certain emphasis on the individual as an American.

Even the Declaration of Independence and the Bill of Rights of the Constitution put this individualism into the legal and common law foundation of how we are to operate in this country.

Duty to society is also part of our American upbringing and cultural education. Certain of the Bill of Rights, Constitutional Amendments, have been modified by the Court rulings to tamper individual rights with the needs of society. For example, the First Amendment, Freedom of Speech, is modified such that you can't shout "Fire" in a crowded theatre if it is not true. The individual rights mitigated for the good of society as a whole.

Nevertheless, individual freedoms are so ingrained into the social psychology of the American voter's brain, when a politician speaks to "loss of individual freedoms" that kicks up an awakened diligence response, much like a survival "fight or flight response" in many voters. Then, the next things said will slide more easily into the person's brain as acceptable and a valid interpretation of the situation at hand.

Note that I am saying that the **mere mention** of the terms "Freedom" or "restrictions on Freedom" shift the brain into an (unconscious) fear/survival mode at the deep brain level. Then the rational mind kicks in and the next thing a politician may say has a better chance of being accepted as true. When you read the text of the Ted Cruz speech at Liberty University later in this book you will see how often applause responses occur. Staged or not, these applause responses are an emotional outburst and reaction that warms the potential voter to like the speaker. If not forever, at least for a short time.

Both Ted Cruz and Donald Trump use this phraseology over and over again, as if by saying it it makes them more American than others. More trustworthy than others. More Presidential than those that don't say it over and over again.

Listen to the Presidential speeches from the Oval Office. For decades the ending of almost all of those speeches invoke Freedom and the Blessings of God on the American people.

Say the same thing as a candidate and you sound more Presidential (if the person/voter listening actually listens to any Presidential speeches).

Invoking what you can do for society and societal obligations are also part of American education and even part of the brain's structure. After all, we are social and tribal beings. President John F. Kennedy's famous line "Ask not what your country can do for you, ask what you can do for your country" is the gold standard for the President invoking societal obligation and patriotism. Asking the American voter to help society, to volunteer for the good of the country, can motivate some voters. But I think that it is not as strong of a sales hook as the former part of the phase, "ask not what your country can do for you" because by removing the "not" we are back to the very powerful radio station, WIFM.

Individualism and self-preservation and self-interest are stronger motivators for most people than is helping the community. However, this statement assumes that the voter is not a NURTURING type. More on this later in the book when discussing the B.A.N.K.™ CODE personality typing system. You can get a hint about this topic by going to www.Four-Cards.com and play theB.A.N.K.™ CODE card game or by looking on page 17 of the White Paper confirming the validity of the B.A.N.K.™ CODE personality coding system. You can also get a copy of the executive summary of the white paper at www.Four-cards.com.

Individual responsibility vs teamwork

Politicians will invoke individual freedom first, and then they will tout the virtues of individual responsibility if they are speaking to a target audience who believes that people need to pick themselves up by their "bootstraps." Voters who think that getting a hand up is a sign of weakness and who think that food stamps, welfare assistance, social security checks, Medicare, and other forms of federal assistance as negative will respond positively to this invocation of the term "individual responsibility."

Granted that we all have individual responsibility for many aspects of our life. We put things in our mouths -- we say things -- we do things to others. American society says that that is both our freedom but also our responsibility when it comes to the law and criminal actions.

However, none of us are born spontaneously. It is a team effort. What do I mean by that? Getting the food we eat is largely a group and team effort. The products were use and rely on -- transportation, clothing, shelter, work place, computers, cell phones, etc. -- are a result of teamwork. And many people going to school or university are there because of scholarships or grants. This is teamwork and also charity from others.

In the arena of politics though, calls for teamwork, charity, community effort, inclusiveness is made by candidates who believe in team work and know that nothing is done in a vacuum. Bernie Sanders has been a vocal advocate of this whereas Donald Trump has been more of the individual responsibility type of candidate. What do we make of the book that Hillary Clinton wrote (with help) "It Takes a Village?" This also is emphasizing the teamwork angle.

On the other hand, some politicians will emphasize the "many "I's" vs the team" idea. That it is the individual who is important in the team and not the synergism. This is more the A-Type in B.A.N.K. ™ CODE.

Other concepts that are subtly promoted in political speeches are the "I versus Us," "Us vs Them," and personal interest vs big picture thinking. This is weighing in on the individualism construct as being most important, and placing the value of other people lower on the neuropsychosocial hierarchy of importance.

This neuropsychosocial hierarchy is as follows:

-- It starts with ME,

-- then it turns to US, the plural of ME,

-- then to the Team, (ME and others)

-- and then to Them/Others (the not ME or US)

This is another way of saying that everyone listens first to WIFM. Later on, if they mature in their listening behaviors, they graduate on to WIFU, WIFT, and WIFO (what's in it for OTHERS - and how can I help them).

Individual Responsibility vs Collective Cooperation

This subtitle is just another way of phrasing the dichotomies of "Individual versus Society," "Individual versus Government," and "Individual Responsibility versus

Teamwork." Thankfully I already addressed this previously.

Aren't you relieved to not have yet another overly pedantic faux-academic diatribe to decipher? BTW, politicians try to use small words, aimed at the 6th grader education level,. That is because they don't want to lose your attention on a word you may not know. When you don't know a word you start to focus on that word to figure it out. Thus, you are no longer listening to them and they want to be in control of the conversation, so you'll never hear them talking about things like antidisestablishmentarianism.

Values versus Policy:

All humans individually, and as a culture, hold certain values. The greater the commonality, the greater the cohesiveness of the culture. The more diverse the values held and practiced, the more potential for conflict but also perhaps greater innovation. The population of the United States has a huge diversity of religions, races, countries-of-origin, and native tongues. Even the Native American population is diverse in culture and language. How does a politician speak to the diversity of her or his constituents and still get elected?

Once again, the most persuasive political candidates know how to sell. Politicians have sales acumen as their currency.

The sales may be fund-raising abilities, creating teams of people who will volunteer for them, or of captivating the imagination of the party machinery. But, they always have to be selling to survive in politics. (Did you catch that I said this before? I did because it is important to understand.)

Sales have to occur to win an election. You have to show that you, as the candidate, have sufficient value to the voter for her or him to take the time to vote.

So value here refers to the value of the candidate to the voter.

Another meaning of "values" is illustrated by the following words that people believe in: Freedom, Independence, Individualism, Charity, Education, Integrity, Personal Growth, Trust in Relationships, Fairness, Consistency, Loyalty, Religious beliefs (including having no religious belief), Pursuit of Happiness, Privacy, etc. Values are beliefs that are important to people and guide them in their behavior and decision making.

Values and beliefs are so deeply integrated into a person's personality that politicians know that speaking to a person's values, as well as to their fears and aspirations, is the way to a person's heart, vote, and even pocketbook.

Policies are the principles that will guide a candidate in deciding how to carry out activities in a consistent and step-by-step fashion. Policies imply continuity, not arbitrarily. But, policies are less immediate to most voters; values, which evoke a deeper emotional response, are a more immediate channel to winning over a voter. Policies are more logic and rationality based. Values are more emotionally based.

The old maxim goes: Emotion sells and Logic Justifies (the purchase or choice). So a successful candidate pushes emotional buttons first and then follows it up with a little rationality.

Values can be divisive. But when a candidate choses a universal value, like "survival," everyone listens even if they don't want to. If the candidate chooses a less basic survival value, like personal growth or consistency, they will be speaking to a smaller part of the population. Their voting base has narrowed. But they don't have to get 100% of the ears at any one time to win the election.

The "3 H's"

Americans vote with their heads, hearts, and hopes. The so-called "3 H's" - (not to be confused with the venerable "4-H Clubs" of agricultural America). No matter what they may say during presidential primary or general election polls, in the voting booth voters ultimately have to make a decision and that usually is based on values. Values are based on beliefs and beliefs are based on feelings and thoughts.

So, when a voter doesn't have a candidate choice on the ballot who they clearly like, they have to prioritize and choose "the lesser of two (or more) evils." Which one do you despise less? Which one is not as bad? Which one doesn't turn your stomach as much? Face it, VOTER, either you hold your nose and vote anyway or you make a choice and do not vote for either (any) candidate. You choose by not choosing – by skipping that check box, lever, or chad.

One reason for this dilemma is the fact that "ranked voting" is
not instituted in the U.S. Body politic. In other words, you
can't rank your choices from 1 to 5, with your ability to really
vote for who you want to win put at #1. Then you rank on
down in choices. The dilemma of having to make a Yes/No
vote is that if you vote only for the "dark horse" candidate
you might ultimately end up allowing someone else to win
who you want to strongly vote against.

In short, many people don't vote in presidential and other
elections is because ranked voting does not exist in almost all
U.S. elections.

Why not you ask? Because the political parties are dead set
against this in almost every election cycle precisely because
they know that 3 rd. or 4 th party candidates would get so
many more votes. This would show the weakness of the two
major parties. And so the Democratic and Republican parties
can't allow their power to be eroded.

The two major political parties will do anything to prevent an
erosion of their power, even if that means creating an

"apathetic" electorate. Political pundits claim that the electorate, the eligible voters, don't vote because they are apathetic and just don't care. The reality is quite the opposite.

Voters care so much they vote by not voting. It may sound like a contradiction, but they cast a vote of no-confidence by saying "I don't think my vote counts anyway so I will not take the time or effort to cast a ballot for candidates I don't believe in." The bottom line (in this section on "Values vs Policy") is this: voters have feelings about political candidates. The feelings create beliefs. The beliefs are the basis of values. And the voter looks at the political candidates or politicians and they then judge what that person's values really are. And then they vote based on their perception of values, personality, integrity, intelligence, honesty, etc. that those candidates display.

Various Miscellaneous Other Determinants of Voting

Other political psychology factors that play into deciding what the candidates' values are include:

--what policies they espouse,

--what policies they have historically supported,

--their historical record regarding jobs, crimes, marriages, children, divorces, and scandals,

--content of previous speeches,

--mea calpas,

--what their party is and which faction of the party they align with, if any

--their other actions in life,

--how they look,

--how they dress,

--how they carry themselves,

--how tall they are,

--how does their voice sound – do they want to listen to that voice for 4 – 8 years?

--what color their skin is,

--what they say their religion is or isn't,

-etc. etc.

Addressing the Reptilian in us All (the Survival Brain): Food Clothing and Shelter

Once again we are touching on the survival brain. The so-called reptilian brain because even reptiles have this kind of a brain/nervous system structure.

Don't think that I am calling humans or Americans snakes, crocodiles or turtles. It is simply that all of us, including the homeless, hungry and "shabbily dressed" need the basics that are taught to all elementary school children in geography or social studies. The BIG THREE survival basics: Food, clothing, and shelter. People need some way to get cash flow or economic exchange for that to happen. It doesn't happen anymore just living off the land. So some might include that "needing a job" for all of the above is number 4 in the survival basics list. Without a means of producing some cash flow, poverty, unemployment, high debt load, etc. are the results.

Thus, these are topics that politician speak about, and make promises to address, to the voters. Whether you paint a pretty picture of the dream you will fulfill for the American worker or the debt-riddled university graduate, or you say that you will "make America great again," vague terms or specific policies and plans are the "tellings" that politicians say to address the survival brain of the voters.

Thus, these are topics that politicians speak about, and make promises to address, to the voters. Whether you paint a pretty picture of the dream you will fulfill for the American worker or the debt-riddled university graduate, or you say that you will "make America great again," vague terms or specific policies and plans are the "tellings" that politicians say to address the survival brain of the voters.

Fear vs Confidence

People respond to confidence. The often follow a leader, even on a hike with friends, if that person seems more confident than they are. Scare them and show them you are confident. Trigger the fear/survival response mechanism and then engage the "tribal need" / "belonging" part of the brain. Shower them with flowering generalities of a better tomorrow.

It is surprising how often it works at least in the short term.

Do it often enough and maybe they will vote for you on
Election Day. Some people also may have heard me say
"confidence is a placebo for rational observation."

This also works when starting with fear and then invoking
ideas of freedom, individuality and even charity. Adding in
the element of competition with the "enemy" and the need to
"win" also touches on the survival instincts. Making the issue
a "friends or foe" dichotomy can also be a very effective entry
into the support psychology of the voter.

Recognizing threats -- creating false threats and false enemies

Once again, same old theme. Induce fear, even if you know it
is false. Then point to the supposed perpetrator of the threat
to take the heat off of yourself. A serious case in point was the
"weapons of mass destruction" argument the George W. Bush
administration had Secretary of Defense Colin Powell push on
the United Nations. There were those who knew this to be
false, but it was pushed and as resulted in untold misery,
death and destruction in Iraq and other parts of the world.

The emergence of ISIS being a likely result of destabilization
induced by invasion and dismantlement of Iraq's dictatorship.

Chapter 6. Archetypes to Understand Human Behavior and Then Speak to It

Observing human behavior, cultures, value systems, and buying/voting patterns

Humans are a rare species, don't you think?

Humans are fascinating, exciting, wonderful, innovating, frustrating, annoying, and everything in between. We are emotional and we are rational.

And we humans like to observe and talk about other humans and their behaviors. We do it over dinner, at lunch, at the "water cooler," on TWITTER, Facebook, in letters, in text messages, on the phone and even on TALK TV. Because behaviors have a huge influence on society as a whole and on each of us as individuals, we spend time trying to understand and predict the behaviors of other people. Would you agree?

For example, you are walking down a crowded sidewalk.

Other people are walking the same direction that you are. But, there are also people walking towards you, going the opposite way that you are walking. When you meet that person face to face you will want to avoid running into them. So, you each move aside to walk past each other and not run into each other full speed ahead. How do you know, predict, which way that person will go?

Well, generally people will go to the right, like traffic. BUT, if you live in Tokyo or London, for example, you will go to the left instead, as that is how people drive in those countries. Depending upon where you are walking, you can predict the walking behavior of others. Sometimes it is an unconscious prediction, other times you have to consciously think about it at each encounter.

I lived in Japan for about 3 year's total. When I went to visit Japan after living in California for many years, I had to consciously think "which way do I move on the sidewalks" because they walk on the opposite side of the sidewalk. Even when the sidewalks were relatively empty, the same rule

applied. And that rule was "move to the left." I got used to that after a day or two in Tokyo. Later on during my travels I went on down to Osaka and Kyoto. Walking up the train

station steps I started running into people again! "What the heck!?? Why are they going to the right here (kabam!)?" I asked my Japanese friends (I speak Japanese) about this. In actuality, people in Osaka and Kyoto walk on the same side of the street as in California! It is the opposite of Tokyo, even though everyone in Japan drives the way they do in England. In other words, the opposite of California and the other parts of the U.S.

I wondered why this was so? I asked my Osaka and Sakai city friends. They smiled, laughed, and said "We like to be different from Tokyo!"

You see, the cultures of the Kansai area of Japan, where Kyoto, Osaka, Sakai and other cities are located are older than that of Tokyo. Tokyo is in the region of Japan called Kantou. Thus, there are regional dialects in Kansai that differ from the "hyojyungo" (Standardized) Japanese of Tokyo, in the Kantou

region. Everyone in Japan knows how to speak Tokyo-style, but in their own regions they have dialects that give them a distinctive culture.

My point here being, we humans still need to predict the behavior of other humans in order to interact and communicate with them. Ideally, we interact and communicate in the way they want to be communicated with. And not everyone behaves or communicates in the same way.

I know. That's obvious. You are saying to yourself "I already know that." If you have done any travel at all you understand what I am saying.

So when it comes to political candidates speaking to the voters, what are the biases that the candidate may have that influence their ability to communicate effectively? What will give them a positive influence and what will kill their chances of getting enough votes? Again, that is the topic of this book.

Behavioral Models Shedding Light on Humans

"Behavioral Models Shedding Light on Humans." That sounds kinda dry and boring, doesn't it? But really, it is just about reality TV, dating shows, and rumor mills. And, it is about the tools that human resource departments, hiring managers, and law enforcement profilers use.

Now are you interested?

People gab about other people. People also speak highly of certain people and put down others. Dr. Phil, Judge Judy, The Bachelor and The Bachelorette, House of Cards, Scandal. All these shows point out the supportive and the back-stabbing nature of human interactions. But they all have people talking about others.

Why we do that? Well, that is not always clear, but our desire to create some ability to get what we want from others is a basic human drive. If we can't survive on our own, we have to figure out how to do it with the help of others. And if they don't help, how can we get them to do it anyway?

"No man is an island."

"It takes a village."

We learn that if we act a certain way then we might get what we want or need. If we act in another way things don't go so well. Maybe we even get punished. But to survive and thrive, we have to sort out the difference between the two.

Sometimes we get help with figuring this out, and sometimes we are left to our own devices. Our role models may be the pattern that helps us succeed, or doing what they do might be the wrong direction. So, learning new and better ways to act and think is always the choice of the resilient person.

What are these "new and better ways?"

Over time, people have devised various models of behavior, or values, or preferences to help them better understand and predict other people's (and their own) behaviors. A few of these models include Meyers-Briggs, Enneagram, Astrological Systems (Western, Ayurvedic, Chinese, etc.), Numerology, D.I.S.C.™ and B.A.N.K. ™ CODE.

These and many other models are used for various purposes:

- predicting the best time to have a wedding,
- deciding the best foods someone should eat based on their constitution,
- what kind of job or relationship a person is best suited for,
- and even how to best sell to other people.

It is this last category that we explore here. Sales. How we can use behavioral models to sell to others.

B.A.N.K. ™ CODE

WORDS OF CAUTION & DISCLAIMER NOTE: The author is a
Certified Trainer with BANKCODE. He has had years of
experience in coding patients, salespersons, marketers, other
business people, family and friends. However, with respect to
these findings and opinions in this book, he does not speak for
BANKCODE, B.A.N.K. ™ CODE ACADEMY, or any other
person associated with B.A.N.K. ™ Code. The analysis and
interpretations of the data are the sole opinion of the author.
The data come from other willing volunteers, almost all of
whom could be eligible voters. This is in no way an official or
even unofficial position or opinion or suggestion of the
BANKCODE Company, GLOBAL XTS or its principals. It is
just a fun study by a KNOWLEDGE type, the author of this
book. Also, none of the candidates or politicians mentioned in
this book have actually done their B.A.N.K. ™ CODE, and that
is the only definitive way to say what their B.A.N.K. ™ CODE
might be.

So, what are the 4 B.A.N.K. ™ CODE personality types? Based
on page 4 of the Executive Summary of the white paper, the
following are some basic values associated with each of the
four validated personality codes.

BLUEPRINT, ACTION, NURTURING, and KNOWLEDGE.

And some of the basic values associated with them?

BLUEPRINT: Stability, Structure, Tradition, Following Rules, Credentials

ACTION: Image, Opportunity (including Money with a capital "M"), Winning, Competition, Excitement, Attention (All about ME), Freedom, and Spontaneity

NURTURING: Relationships, Community, Teamwork, Ethics, Harmony and Charity. (Service to others)

KNOWLEDGE: Learning, Technology, Intelligence, the Big Picture, Science, Logic

You can find out what your own BLUEPRINT, ACTION, NURTURING, and KNOWLEDGE B.A.N.K. ™ CODE is by going to http://www.Four-cards.com and playing the card game by clicking the link embedded in the top logo. Or click a link farther down in the text related to B.A.N.K. PASS ™.

The thing is, each one of us has all four of the personality types in us to some degree. For some of us, one or two predominate, in others there is more of a balance. When we think of other's code, sometimes the predominant one jumps out at us. Other times the first or even second one are less clear.

So by looking at just the briefest of explanations of the above B.A.N.K. ™ CODE types, do you think that my classification of the primary following person's B.A.N.K. ™ CODE type is accurate?

- Typing past Presidents: Ronald Regan (BNAK), Eisenhower (B), Lyndon Banes Johnson (A), John F Kennedy (ANKB)
- Typing past presidential candidates
  Al Gore (K),
  Ross Perot (K)
  Carlie Fiorina (K)
  Barry Goldwater (B)
  Jeb Bush (NB)
  Ted Cruz (B)
  Ralph Nader (K)

Neurolinguistic Programming NLP

Another important model of understanding human behavior and then communicating effectively is a technology called Neurolinguistic Programming NLP. The basic premise is that we all use five senses to understand the world around us. Sight, hearing, touch/feeling, smell and taste. We respond to all five, but in modern society the first three predominate. And each of us may have a predominant one even among those 3. Maybe we are more visually alert. Or we respond to

sounds more. Or maybe we are more emotional and remember and respond to emotions more. Our life may revolve around how we feel about others and less about how they look.

Our experience of life is shaped by our senses. Our experience of politicians is shaped by how we sense them. How well a politician can communicate in all of the sensory modes effects how well they can influence our thinking and either get us on their side or repel us.

In the most basic terms, the more they can paint the picture, invoke the sounds, and move our emotions IN WORDS and actions the more likely they will reach all types of people. Thom Hartmann does a great job of explaining this in more detail in his book listed at the end of this book.

As an aware voter, this is something you should be aware of while listening to and watching a politician who is moving and motivating you into action.

Chapter 7: Selling Techniques for the American Voter:

How do the candidates, and even sitting politician, sell to the American voter? Of course, by combining all of the things we have discussed in the chapter on voter psychology. Whether designed by purpose or by prophetic accident, all candidates have a clear purpose in their communications with the electorate or their constituents. Just review all the things talked about in Chapter 4 and 5 and you will be able to analyze any speech, article, newsletter, or social media post from the candidates.

It is important to remember that no candidate will win all votes. They know that, we know that. A 100% winning election would raise red flags. Politicians are gamblers as well as sellers. They know the odds of their winning any particular race, and they do what they can to improve their odds.

Improving the Odds of Winning the Presidency

One method is to create a strong like or dislike reaction. You deliberately speak to and create your tribe. You speak with this attitude: either you like me or hate me. Make it clear where you stand (Mr. or Ms Electorate). You decide if you are in my tribe or not. Ultimately, the voter is going to have to decide in the voting booth, on an absentee ballot, or in a party caucus.

If the candidate creates a strong impression, shows confidence, at least the voter can react. And reaction is emotion. And emotion can lead to action. If a candidate creates no emotional reaction, they have lost the first chance to get a vote. Because most voters want clarity, they want a candidate that can be decisive. Or do you disagree, and think that the ambiguous candidate is the one you are attracted to?

And if voters wants a decisive president, do they want one that makes snap judgments based on emotional reactions, or a president who weighs all the options, looks at the big picture, and ponders awhile all the information before making a decision? Do they want a shoot from the hip president, or one who lines everything up, figures the wind speed and all other factors, and then pulls the trigger?

A good story always helps. Integrating visual, auditory, and kinesthetic elements awakens the human brain and makes a story come alive. That's also why movies and sizzle reels work so well to sell a concept of a candidate. That's why a great story is used to sell products.

In short, selling to the American voter is perhaps complicated, but if you are able to get the eye and ear of the voters at least you have a better chance of winning than if you are a total unknown. Word of mouth and some media coverage if essential. That is no different than selling anything. At this point let me prematurely describe some survey results detailed in Chapter 9. It might make sense or no sense to you. The next chapter clarifies a bit more.

Chapter 8: CODE BLUE or CODE RED in the White House? Current Presidential Candidates

When you hear the phrase "Code Blue" what do you think of? Many people who are TV watchers of medical shows might conjure up the thought "Someone's heart has stopped. They are turning blue. The resuscitation team needs to get to them very quickly or they might really die.

Others might think, "Oh, Code Blue in the White House. Must mean something about the death of the Presidency." or "The President in the White House is going to die." or, reading even more into the phrase, "The Presidents who were assassinated all were ones who were advocating for a National Bank."

Then again, everyone also knows about the phrase "Code Red." This means an emergency. Maybe an international conflict has gotten so bad the military is on high alert and the use of nuclear weapons is being considered. Or a natural disaster has become so bad, like a major hurricane, that a national disaster is declared. At any rate, "Code Red" is a dangerous situation. But the title is not "Code Red in the White House." It is "Code Blue in the White House." So, why else may the title have been called Code Blue?

Well, political pundits might be thinking that the traditional colors associated with the Republican and Democratic parties are somehow involved in this Code Blue title, suggesting that the Democrats (the "blue states") will be in the White House again after the 8 years of the Democratic Obama Presidency.

WORDS OF CAUTION & DISCLAIMER NOTE: The author a Certified Trainer with BANKCODE. He has had years of experience in coding patients, salespersons, marketers, other business people, family and friends. However, with respect to these findings and opinions in this book, he does not speak for BANKCODE, B.A.N.K. ™ CODE ACADEMY, or any other person associated with B.A.N.K. ™ Code. The analysis and interpretations of the data are the sole opinion of the author. The data come from other willing volunteers, almost all of whom could be eligible voters. This is in no way an official or even unofficial position or opinion or suggestion of the

BANKCODE Company, GLOBAL XTS or its principals. It is just a fun study by a KNOWLEDGE type, the author of this book.

Blue is associated in the B.A.N.K. ™ CODE personality testing system with a BLUEPRINT type. Blueprints are plans to be followed. They are a traditional architectural tool. They create the structure that must be followed to create a reliable building, a box that someone can live or work in safely.

The BLUEPRINT type of personality likes titles and uniforms. They believe in hierarchies. The military is a good example of the values associated with the BLUEPRINT type. And the military, as well as the military-industrial complex is known to command a huge part of the U.S. government budget. The President is the Commander in Chief of the Military, so the influence of the military in the White House is very significant from the standpoint of titling this book "Code Blue."

The question arises, who would the military industrial complex want to be in the White House? Obviously they want someone who would represent their needs and values, which include having as big of a budget as they want, having solid pension plans and veteran's benefits, and having support to protect the lives of solders and commanders by not conducting frivolous wars or interventions. Democratic or Republican objectively is not a huge issue for the military in reality because they have not had huge problems getting support from either party (although the downsizing that occurred in the past after the end of the Cold War was met with resistance from many quarters, not just the uniformed military but also the civilian defense industries). Both Democrats and Republicans were involved in downsizing as was the military itself. The military had to come up with the lists of priorities of things like base closings.

The bottom line with the "Code Blue" innuendo is that all of the above meanings and suggestions are relevant for the title of this book.

-- Is a death or assassination of a president in the future?

-- Is the military a controlling factor in the selection of the President?

-- Is it necessary for a candidate to be a heavy backer of
military intervention to be elected?

-- Is a Republican or a Democrat going to ascend to the
Presidency this time around?

So, given that long introduction to this chapter, which
presidential candidate is most likely to get into the Code Blue
White House? Who will win the White House?

Most people would agree that the Republican Party is most
often associated with putting forward a part platform that
brags that they have a stronger support for the military than
do the Democrats. People generally would say that
Republicans are more traditional and conservative than
Democrats. Of course, there is the predominance of the "Blue
Dog" Democrats in the past few decades that fades that
distinction between the Republicans and Democrats.
Interesting that they chose the term "BLUE Dogs."

I will go into greater depth on explaining personality types in
a later chapter, but this cycle of presidential hopefuls has been
particularly intriguing this time. Because the traditional
conservative candidate representing the Republican Party,

having a lot of BLUEPRINT characteristics, is surprisingly absent. Ted Cruz, Marco Rubio, a couple of others who ran are definitely in the BLUEPRINT dominant arena. Donald Trump is definitely not much of a BLUEPRINT. He doesn't operate within the "box." So there was a definite Republican rejection of this outsider from the start. He is not sufficiently "Code Blue."

As you will see later as well, even Barack Obama and Hillary Clinton are more Blue than Donald Trump. And for the Republicans who really want a Code Blue in the White House, the thought that Hillary Clinton is more of their candidate than Donald Trump is turning the stomachs of the Republican leadership. This is well evidenced by the outright rejection of Donald Trump as a candidate for the Republicans by the Republicans from the start. There is still a begrudging acceptance by negotiation of a slim majority of Republican leaders at this point. Republican Presidents have even stated that they were not going to attend the Republican Convention. Has this ever happened before?

So, before you read on about Personality types, I ask that you participate in a survey of your opinion on the personality types of the past Presidents, past presidential candidates, and current presidential candidates.

Which type do you think each candidate predominantly fits? Before going on, give your opinion in our national poll. Go to http://www.SurveyMonkey.com/r/Presidential-Survey. Please participate in this survey to see how your ideas fit with the surveys we have in this book. You will also qualify to get a discount on your own personality analysis by completing this survey.

SUMMARY: When surveys are done on the candidates, how quickly people can decide which candidate fits what B.A.N.K. ™ CODE depends upon two possibilities: either a quick recognition of values or a confusion about what values they hold.

So at this point, let me prematurely describe some survey results that may or may not make sense to you. The next chapter clarifies a bit more, but here we go.

My surveys revealed the following:

1. All successful Presidents of the past were a mixture of
    B.A.N.K. ™ CODE types, and most had at least a little
    Nurturing in them.

2. All Republicans had strong BLUEPRINT, with Barack
    Obama, a Democrat, having the most BLUEPRINT of
    any president. I believe that this explains why he may
    have won his two elections with some Republican
    votes. It also suggests why many Republicans vilified
    him so much.

3. Donald Trump – almost all people, novices or experts
    on B.A.N.K. ™ CODE immediately said he was an A
    type – only one said he was a B type. I think that he
    doesn't have enough B type in him intrinsically to
    appeal to Republicans. Perhaps knowing this he tried
    to use Sarah Palin (B and A type) to enhance his
    BLUEPRINT, but her lack of intellectual focus detracted
    from his message. (This is not to say that I think Donald
    Trump had a particularly focused message in the first
    three quarters of his campaign other than tearing down
    everyone else.)

4. On the other hand, the satire that ensued from the Palin endorsement was just more publicity and free air time

5. for the Donald.

6. This recognition of his uber-A-typeness even was found when I surveyed Japanese citizens in Sakai-City, Japan during a student exchange in August. (I am actually in Nagasaki on the Memorial Day of the atomic bombing, paying my respects and finishing up my writing as we speak.) Even Pilipino here in Nagasaki who are involved in a peace summit also chose the A-card as Donald Trump's primary code.

7. Approximately one in ten respondents have initially said that Donald Trump doesn't fit any of the cards because none of the cards list negative characteristics.

8. Bernie Sanders – most said N type, but a few said he was a K type. He doesn't have enough BLUEPRINT to have the Code Blue endorsement. And he displayed only minimal values of Action in the first position -- much more being a team work and community/service oriented campaign than a "Me Me Me" campaign. Same results in Japan.

9. Hillary Clinton – there was confusion by many, whether she was K or B type, a few said N and one said A. Same thing in Japan.

10. It seems more and more clear over time that anyone with such an unclear mix of types creates confusion in the electorate. Past Democratic Presidents have had a mixture of types. And Hillary Clinton's profile seems close to that of President Barack Obama. Hillary Clinton's support for the White House thus is, first and foremost, her primary tribe. Then, like all presidential election winners, a win will turn out to hinge on Democratic operatives, Democratic loyalists looking for jobs and political favors, and people who feel a woman should be elected to the Presidency sometime. And then there is the alternative. So compared to Donald Trump, why not now?

Chapter 9: Research on Presidential Personality Typing

General Comments

In previous chapters we talked about values, the psychology of voters, imprinting, and a variety of other aspects of the election of presidents by voters who have been convinced that that candidate is the person they want to choose. Or at least that candidate is less terrible than the other one(s).

People tend to trust people who are like them in many ways. When people have similar personalities they mesh more easily. That doesn't mean that they don't ever clash, because they can and do when they are very much alike. Especially when they are very competitive and winning is everything.

The bottom line is that personality typing IS a powerful predictor of behavior. Thus, using the B.A.N.K. ™ personality coding system to see how it might be able to predict behavior was an experiment I wanted to try out. B.A.N.K. ™ code personality typing has been helpful in many businesses and relationships to create win-win sales. We know also, based on a recent scientific and academic study of B.A.N.K. ™ personality coding system that it can help to predict buying behavior. Voting for a candidate is "buying" that candidate. The candidate convinced the voter to spend time and money to take the action of voting. That is a sale.

One of the geniuses of the B.A.N.K. ™ personality coding system is the use of 4 cards that a person stacks from most important to least important to that person. I have done this at least 400 or more times and only 1 time did someone refuse. That person relented later when others around him readily agreed to play the cards. The fact that that refuser was "autistic" may or may not have also been a factor in initial suspicion and reluctance.

I mention my experience with B.A.N.K. ™ personality code card sorting because, while it is not always easy for someone to stack them according to importance, people get the meaning and eventually come up with their answer to "the game," and that it happens in less than 90 seconds.

As a Certified Trainer with BANKCODE, I have spent years studying the Four Types and have taken many classes, including the SPEEDCODING™ class where we practiced trying to get all 4 codes of a person in the right order just by asking questions and observing. This takes some practice and focus, believe me. The point is, I have had the great honor and opportunity to be around many experts in B.A.N.K. ™ coding as well.

So, I know B.A.N.K. ™ Code from the perspective of the newbie, the person who has never seen the cards before, and also from the perspective of the expert. I wanted to see how consistent both groups might be in assessing the predominant B.A.N.K. ™ Code type of the current candidates and past presidents.

You, the reader can participate in this on-going study as well by going to the following website and complete my survey. http://www.surveymonkey.com/r/Presidential_Survey . Please give me your insights as well.

But, while the numbers in this study are not statistically significant so far, the results are in keeping with my own initial, personal impressions of what the predominant B.A.N.K.™ Code type is for these politicians.

So, first I will present the decision of "The People." The "newbies." Next I compare it with the aggregate impressions by 10 experts. Then I make some bold statements interpreting these results in terms of the viability of candidates and who will win the 2016 election.

WORDS OF CAUTION & DISCLAIMER NOTE: The author is a Certified Trainer with BANKCODE. He has had years of experience in coding patients, salespersons, marketers, other business people, family and friends. However, with respect to these findings and opinions in this book, he does not speak for BANKCODE, B.A.N.K. ™ CODE ACADEMY, or any other person associated with B.A.N.K. ™ Code. The analysis and interpretations of the data are the sole opinion of the author. The data come from other willing volunteers, almost all of whom could be eligible voters. This is in no way an official or even unofficial position or opinion or suggestion of the BANKCODE Company, GLOBAL XTS or its principals. It is just a fun study by a KNOWLEDGE type, the author of this book.

Chart of "The Peoples" Quick Impression on Candidate Personality Types (6-30-16 update)

	Informal Poll of Personality Types			
	Action	*Nurturer*	*Blueprint*	*Knowledge*
At JFK	Trump	Bernie	Hillary	
University	Trump	Bernie		Hillary
	Trump	Bernie	Hillary	Hillary
By Office				Trump / Hillary
Patients	Hillary		Trump	Bernie
	Trump	Bernie	Cruz	Hillary
	Trump	Bernie/Obama		Hillary / Obama
	Trump		Hillary	
	Trump	? Bernie 2 Hillary	Hillary	Bernie
	Trump	Hillary?		Bernie
	Trump	Bernie		Hillary
	Trump	Bernie	Trump	Hillary
	Trump	Bernie	Hillary / Cruz	
	Trump	Bernie	Hillary	
		Summary		
Trump	**Action = 12**	Nurturer = 0	Blueprint = 2	Knowledge = 1
Hillary	Action = 1	Nurturer = 2	Blueprint = 6	**Knowledge = 7**
Bernie	Action = 0	**Nurturer = 10**	Blueprint = 0	Knowledge = 3
Cruz	Action = 0	Nurturer = 0	**Blueprint = 2**	Knowledge = 0
Obama	Action = 0	Nurturer = 1	Blueprint = 0	Knowledge = 1

What the "Newbies" Think

In summary, the above chart shows the results of my informal poll of people just introduced to the BANKCODE value cards. When asked "which is the predominant value card" of each candidate, this is the response with respect to the order of the frequency of cards selected for each candidate. (The chart results don't add up evenly in all cases as some people didn't opine on particular candidates they didn't know.)

These results are the impressions we have. We don't know what order the candidates themselves would put the value cards in. Of course, I would love to hand them the cards and ask them to rank the cards. Like everyone else, I am sure that they would do it readily!

But, because this has not happened, these conclusions are just an inkling of the perceived B.A.N.K. ™ Codes of presidential candidates from "random individuals," the "people on the street." On the chart, the top three survey results were done by employees or professors in a university. The 9 at the bottom were patients I surveyed at a natural medicine practice in Berkeley, California – The Redwood Clinic. All of the "candidate" impressions were made often after the person had just played the B.A.N.K. ™ Code cards with respect to themselves.

<u>NOTE on 4-letter Word Nomenclature Used in this Research
Study:</u> The 4 letter combination at the end of the line is the
shorthand we use in BANKCODE training to designate the
order of the sorted cards. When you play the cards normally
(www.Four-Cards.com) you stack and choose to put ALL 4
cards in order. However, here, I asked people to just choose
the predominant card. Thus, they chose just one card and not
4 (although a couple of people did put all 4 in order).   Thus,
because I asked people to choose only ONE card, not all of the
4 cards might have been selected as the primary code of the
person. Thus, there could be some cards not chosen.

I then had to make up a new system to represent this
situation. Therefore, when there is a "0" (zero) after the
tabulated results for a particular Code-type, that card will go
to the bottom of the card stack. If there are multiple zeros or
there are "ties" between two or more cards, the order of those
cards is not exactly known, so I will put in some possible card
stack results at the end of the line. Or a series of question
marks ("?").

Thoroughly confused yet? Just look below and I'm sure you
will catch on quickly.

So, these are the B.A.N.K. ™ value card stacks according to the "person on the street."

<u>Donald Trump</u>: ACTION (12) BLUEPRINT (2) KNOWLEDGE (1) NURTURING (0)   ABKN

<u>Hillary Clinton</u>: KNOWLEDGE (7) BLUEPRINT (6) ACTION (2) NURTURING (1) KBAN

<u>Bernie Sanders</u>: NURTURING (10) KNOWLEDGE (3) ACTION (0) BLUEPRINT (0) NKAB, or NKBA

<u>Ted Cruz</u>: BLUEPRINT (2) ACTION (0), KNOWLEDGE (0) NURTURING (0) B___

<u>Barack Obama</u>: NURTURING (1), KNOWLEDGE (1), NURTURING (0), ACTION (0) NK__ or KN__

As you can see, the numbers of responses are not statistically significant, and not all of the politicians were carded by everyone. Nevertheless, the results are interesting to me.

Two of the candidates are seen as having really predominant code types.

These were Donald Trump and Bernie Sanders.

These results suggest that on first blush Donald Trump is overwhelmingly an ACTION Type with a little BLUEPRINT and KNOWLEDGE. NOT a NURTURING. As a very strong A-type (ACTION Type) it's all about Donald, with little policy or rules to mix in. Lots of "outside the box" behavior.

Bernie Sanders, on the other hand, is predominantly a NURTURING with some KNOWLEDGE. This is the person who cares about taking care of others.

Hillary Clinton is primarily KNOWLEDGE with BLUEPRINT next, with a little ACTION and NURTURING. This suggests to me that she has a bit more blend, but the KNOWLEDGE and BLUEPRINT types can be a bit stiff when it comes to dealing with people.

At least until the official publication date of this edition of the book in late-August, 2016, I personally have felt that she is more on the intellectual than the emotional end of the continuum. On the other hand, Trump and Sanders are much more emotional, but coming from opposite sides of certain spectrums, namely, the WIFM versus the WIFO perspectives. (See Chapter 2)

Ted Cruz is BLUEPRINT, following the rules, conservative values of tradition. His style of speech is also not flamboyant.

And President Barack Obama is KNOWLEDGE and NURTURING. He is more policy oriented but cares about other people as well. It is interesting to me that in the 2008 election, Hillary Clinton and Barack Obama faced each other in the Democratic Primary, both of them predominantly KNOWLEDGE types (at least according to the Newbies).

B.A.N.K. ™ Code Experts' Opinions

As I mentioned above, in contrast to the "newbies," I recently handed out a more complicated survey at a training for B.A.N.K. ™ CODE trainers. Like myself, these professionals have been using the B.A.N.K. ™ Code personality system

from a few months to several years. They are not "fresh look" "first blush" analyzers. They have even taken the SPEEDCODING™ class, mentioned before, where they get 1 minute to determine all 4 codes in a row, sometimes with remarkable accuracy. I myself did quite well but was not one of the class prize winners. :(

In this exciting and in-depth SPEEDCODING™ class we had to do coding without prior knowledge of who the person is, how they are self-categorized by B.A.N.K.™ code, and without the assistance of the B.A.N.K.™ value cards. (If interested in the SPEEDCODING™ class, learn more by contacting me or by going to http://www.Four-Cards.com)

So, in that class I took, there was my chance to see if the novices are as good at spotting the politicians' primary personality characteristics as the "experts."

Once again, it is good to note that <u>everyone</u> can get even better accuracy by doing the cards. In other words, this means having someone "play the card game" <u>themselves</u>. However, as I mentioned remorsefully a few paragraphs above, I haven't had the chance to ask the presidential candidates to do their own B.A.N.K. ™ Code ranking of the cards by importance.

As an aside then, I can't help myself but to ask you, my esteemed reader: if <u>you </u>happen to know the candidates personally, or any of the Presidents, please ask them to play the cards for me, won't you? I await your call!

So back to the background story on this part of the study. In addition, I asked the B.A.N.K. ™ Code Trainers to personality type a wider range of candidates, past presidents, and past presidential candidates. Not everyone opined on every person – not everyone knows every person on the list. And maybe they have heard of the person but don't have a real impression of them. Thus, the numbers don't always add up to the 10 people who participated out of 20 people total who were there and participated in the survey

Who self-selected out of the voting and why? Granted, some stated that they don't follow politics or watch candidates at all. Some were too busy with classwork that they couldn't be bothered. And this was in spite of my bribing them with a copy of one of my two bestselling books on the brain and dementia!!

(Does this also mean that _I_ should never consider running for President if I can only get 50% of a group of peers to vote with their surveys...?)

Results of the Certified Trainer Experts were as follows:

Informal Poll of Personality Types				
Done at a B.A.N.K.™ CODE Trainer Training 6-2016				
	BLUEPRINT	ACTION	NURTURING	KNOWLEDGE
Donald Trump		9		
Hillary Clinton	3	4	1	1
Bernie Sanders	1		6	
Ted Cruz	6	1		
Marco Rubio	1	2	3	4
Ronald Reagan	5	4		
Richard Nixon	5	1	1	
Jimmy Carter	1	1	8	
Bill Clinton	2	7	2	
George HW Bush	6	4		

	BLUEPRINT	ACTION	NURTURING	KNOWLEDGE
Barack Obama	4	1	2	2
Abraham Lincoln	2		3	3
Al Gore	3		3	2
Carly Fiorina	1	4		
Sarah Palin	1	6	1	
John McCain	5	1	1	1

So how about the B.A.N.K. ™ CODE experts' opinions? The above chart lays it out nicely, but here again in print are the comparative results.

Donald Trump: ACTION (9) BLUEPRINT (0) KNOWLEDGE (0) NURTURING (0)   A____

Hillary Clinton: ACTION (4) BLUEPRINT (3) KNOWLEDGE (1) NURTURING (1) ABKN or ABNK

Bernie Sanders: NURTURING (6) BLUEPRINT (1) ACTION (0) KNOWLEDGE (0) NBAK or NBKA

Ted Cruz: BLUEPRINT (6) ACTION (1), KNOWLEDGE (0) NURTURING (0) BAKN or B.A.N.K. ™

Barack Obama: BLUEPRINT (4), NURTURING (2), KNOWLEDGE (2), ACTION (1) BNKA or BKNA

So do the "newbies" and the "experts" agree or disagree?

They agree that Donald Trump is primarily an A-type. ABKN ("newbies"), and A??? (Experts). Donald Trump is consistently and obviously an ACTION Type, with no one saying he is a NURTURING and the minority saying he is a BLUEPRINT. If we combine all the results of both groups together his score is:

Donald Trump: ACTION (21) BLUEPRINT (2) KNOWLEDGE (1) NURTURING (0)   ABKN

The next most consistent comparative opinion is that of Bernie Sanders. Again, Bernie Sanders is clearly thought to have a predominant Type, that of NURTURING. The person who cares about others more than themselves. The combined score for Bernie Sanders is:

Bernie Sanders: NURTURING (16) KNOWLEDGE (3) BLUEPRINT (1) ACTION (0) NKBA

A comparison of the composite "Speed Coding" types show that Trump and Sanders are exact opposites. ABKN (Trump) and NKBA (Sanders). I think everyone would agree with this impression of the two men. And both being the emotional candidates, they speak to the emotions of the voter. What did we say about sales? "Emotions sell and logic justifies."

Next, in discussing the realm of clarity of the front-running candidates (as of July 4, 2016), is Hillary Clinton. Here the clarity and agreement starts to break down. Both groups agree that in the second place of composite coding, Hillary is a BLUEPRINT. The disagreement occurs more in what is her primary type. Is it KNOWLEDGE as the "newbies" think or ACTION as the "experts" think? The key significance of this for me, and this is strictly my opinion, is that I think that Hillary Clinton is not easy to figure out. (My Japanese friends in Sakai-City in August also said the same thing.) When we do the combined score for her we get:

<u>Hillary Clinton</u>: BLUEPRINT (9) KNOWLEDGE (8) ACTION (6) and NURTURING (2) \ BKAN

So the two groups came up with an amalgamation of BKAN -- from a KBAN (newbies) and ABKN (experts).

Democrats and Republicans: Do They Have a Predominant Code?

This brings me to the next observation on the experts' opinions of Past Presidents. When you look at those results, the Republicans -- Ronald Reagan, Richard Nixon, and George HW Bush -- all were predominantly BLUEPRINT types.

If we compare the archetypical impressions of Republicans and Democrats, most Americans and political pundits would agree that the Republican Party identifies more with the BLUEPRINT type while the Democrats would be identified more with the NUTURINGS.

I believe that it is accurate to say that *Republicans would say that Democrats* spend money they don't have and Republicans are the fiscal conservatives. That perception, while not really true in action, does match up with the BLUEPRINT and NURTURING relative to money. (To learn more in depth about these codes you can order courses by clicking on the appropriate links at www.Four-Cards.com.)

Similarly, I can safely venture to say that *Democrats would say that Democrats* are more concerned about taking care of the middle class and the needy and the Republicans are concerned about the rich and cutting taxes. This also fits with the NURTURINGS and BLUEPRINT characteristics. The BLUEPRINTS having tight-fisted money and budgeting values.

So, Bernie Sanders would be considered more of an archetypical Democrat while Hillary Clinton would be considered more of a Republican! (I think that I discussed the Blue Dog Democrats already.) Donald Trump doesn't have

much BLUEPRINT showing so that might be why the
Republicans have had difficulty getting behind him -- he is not
a team player and doesn't follow the rules.

On the other hand, Ted Cruz is consistently viewed by the
newbies and the experts as primarily BLUEPRINT. The
combination of BA?? and B??? add up to:

Ted Cruz: BLUEPRINT (8) ACTION (1), KNOWLEDGE (0)
NURTURING (0) or a BA??

So why is Ted Cruz losing? (This passage was written prior to
Donald Trump seizing the Republican nomination, much to
the chagrin of a large number of establishment Republicans.)
Look at the successful Republican Presidents. While they were
first place BLUEPRINTS, they also had some ACTION and
maybe some NURTURING (some expert said Nixon was a
NURTURING...). So, maybe Ted Cruz is just TOO
BLUEPRINT to get the backing of Republicans. And Donald

<u>Trump is too ACTION</u> for the Republicans to come together to support him en masse. This mainstream Republican response to Trump has been a consistent theme from 2015 through August 2016, with the Republican Convention epitomizing the dissonance of Donald Trump and Republican standards.

How about other past Democratic Presidents? President Jimmy Carter was highly NURTURING, Bill Clinton was highly ACTION, and Barack Obama was strongly BLUEPRINT, with a composite (newbie and expert) score of:

<u>Barack Obama</u>: BLUEPRINT (4), NURTURING (3), KNOWLEDGE (3), ACTION (1) BNKA or BKNA

So of all the Democratic Presidents, Barack Obama had the most even spread of characteristics and his ACTION was nowhere near what Bill Clinton's was. Bill Clinton was the most ACTION of all the Past Presidents, but no one seems to be comparing Donald Trump with Bill Clinton.

And how about Marco Rubio. Experts say he is very

KNOWLEDGE and NURTURING. Those are not hallmarks of

successful Republican Presidents. His KNAB typing is not

your typical Republican style with the BLUEPRINT at the end.

Of course, this code might be wrong -- we are still waiting for

Marco Rubio, like the other candidates, to play the B.A.N.K.

™ Code card game at http://www.mybankcode.com/drjay.

Losing Presidential Candidates

I also had the experts think about the losing candidates for

President in the past. Not all of them, but a few that stood out

in my mind as a voter over the past 40 years. OMG! Could I

be THAT YOUNG!?

Al Gore lost to George W. Bush. Al Gore, typed as a BNKA or

a NBKA was a NURTURING BLUEPRINT blend with a

KNOWLEDGE bent to him. His movie "An Inconvenient

Truth" was a KNOWLEDGE type sort of a movie, data driven.

His connection with the beginning of the invention of the

internet is also a very KNOWLEDGE value. He lost to the "good 'ol boy" and the Supreme Court by a very thin, chaddy-hanging margin.

John McCain was a strong BLUEPRINT type with not much ACTION. On the other hand, he had Sarah Palin as his Vice-Presidential running mate in 2008. He lost to Barack Obama.

The very high ACTION type Palin was selected by John McCain, perhaps hoping this his 1 point KNOWLEDGE would make up for her zero KNOWLEDGE typing. (Just kidding, but I couldn't help myself poking fun at Governor Palin and her frequent factual gaffs of which she seemed so proud.)

It is so interesting that one of Donald Trump's first endorsements was by none other than Sarah Palin, both having the strong affinity of being predominantly ACTION types. In the next Chapter I do point out the fodder that their joint appearance created for the comedy shows at that time.

Carly Fiorina ran briefly as the running mate with Ted Cruz in February 2016 right before the Indiana primaries. She had previously been running for the presidency since March 2015 as part of the 17 or more Republican candidates at the time. She also ran for the US Senate as the Republican Candidate in California in 2010. Again, here is a strong ACTION type woman Republican candidate, with a little BLUEPRINT showing up. I personally thought that she was more of a KNOWLEDGE type given her CEO stint for Hewlett Packard, but the experts disagreed.

We will have to see just exactly how the ACTION and BLUEPRINT types dichotomy plays out when running for president as a Republican. The ACTION type women haven't fared well, and the ACTION type Donald Trump also is likely to fail, in my humble opinion. He has the Republican nomination and the last day of the Republican Convention plays on my TV at this very moment. His ACTION type antics and how the pundits and political experts talk about the chaotic structure of this year's convention really are fascinating from my B.A.N.K. ™. Code trainer's perspective.

The B.A.N.K. ™ CODE white paper concluded that a person tended to buy according to their own code type. In other words, a KNOWLEDGE type person chooses a KNOWLEDGE oriented sales presentation; an ACTION type an ACTION oriented presentation, etc. How many American voters are the B., A., N., or K. types? We don't know for sure as not everyone in the U.S. has been B.A.N.K. coded. The white paper, due to the academic demands of statistics, had approximately equal numbers of survey members in each type. My own clinical experience as shown that two thirds of my patient population is NURTURING in the first position.

So, if most of my patients are (first place) N-types, that would suggest they would have the greatest affinity with and NURTURING candidate. You can see how both Clinton and Trump played heavily on the family theme during the conventions when previously neither one was showing lots of NURTURING style elements in their speeches or comments. This is their attempt to show a more balanced "value spread" that will resonate with a wider range of voters. Political commentators are still not convinced that it worked.

At any rate, you can get a copy of the whitepaper by going to: http://www.bankcode.com/drjay/whitepaper. There you can verify how important this typing can be in a sales cycle. And I do call this presidential campaign a "sales pitch fest."

Chapter 10: Presidential Election Cycle Comedy

Getting all the free media coverage you can is a primary goal
of all candidates. Now, that would also include social media
attention. Donald Trump has apparently become the
celebrity candidate who has dominated the broadcast
television media. He knows sensationalism, sound bites,
creating controversy, making outlandish claims, and big doses
of negativity. News and chat talk shows use these generously,
and employing all are key components to get coverage and
good air time in news.

Every election cycle, the Comedy Centrals, Saturday Night
Lives, and Late and Late Late Night talk show hosts feast on
what the political candidates and their handlers do. The more
outlandish, the more fodder for fun. This election season is no
different. And then when Donald Trump was endorsed by
Governor Sarah Palin, OMG! The comedians took off from
the already unbelievable unbelievability of the performance of
Sarah Palin and Donald Trump together in Ames, Iowa.
Stephen Colbert on the Late Show is my source for the latest

political candidate shenanigans because of his unique and hilarious straight-face parody of Donald Trump primarily and the other candidates as well. That master of political comedy never gets old. And if I had cable I might see even more political comedy weekly if not nightly on other comedy shows and on news.

Just what can we learn from the content and style of the candidates' speeches? Can we glean which of the 4 B.A.N.K. ™ types they most project in their proxy personality, their alter-ego policies in the form of a prepared speech? Here is that epic moment in Ames, Iowa and the speech, courtesy of CBSN and Youtube.com https://youtu.be/Mvlm3LKSlpU (Note: 21:10 minutes)

Does How Tall a Comedian Is Make a Difference?
You Decide How Relevant Height Is

Heights of some comedians

W. Kamau Bell	6' 4"	1.94 m
Dave Letterman	6' 2"	1.88 m
Stephen Colbert	5' 11"	1.80 m

Arsenio Hall	5' 11"	1.80 m
Don Reed	5' 11"	1.80 m
Gene Wilder	5' 10"	1.78 m
Chris Rock	5' 10"	1.78 m
Richard Pryor	5' 10"	1.78 m
Rodney Dangerfield	5' 10"	1.78 m
Johnny Carson	5' 10"	1.77 m
Eddie Murphy	5' 9"	1.75 m
Jackie Chan	5' 9"	1.74 m
Lillie Tomlin	5' 8"	1.73 m
Marty Feldman	5' 8"	1.73 m
Goldie Hawn	5' 6"	1.68 m
Don Rickles	5' 6"	1.68 m
Sarah Palin	5' 5.5"	1.65 m
Tina Fey	5' 5.5"	1.64 m
Whoopi Goldberg	5' 5"	1.65 m
Anjelah Johnson	5' 4"	1.63 m

Obviously this is not an exhaustive list of all of the comedians in the world or even in the U.S. It is simply a sample of some of the more well known that I have heard over the years or who have appeared on the silver screen or TV. And, they are people whose heights showed up readily in an internet search.

Now, to come back to the question. Do you see any correlation between how funny they are -- or how influential they are in the comedy industry -- and how tall they are? I sincerely hope not. BUT, all of the Late Show hosts are (or were) taller than I am, so my chances of being the next big Late Show comedy talk show host are likely to be very slim. DRAT!!! <u>Another</u> profession my mother said I would be great at and it just won't pan out....

Chapter 11: Presidential Candidate Speeches and Books:
What they tell us about type and selling.

By now you are able to better spot the values and perspectives
that might characterize speech and behavior of political
candidates in the context of the communication styles and
influence skills. I have included speeches from each of the
major candidates so that you might decide for yourself which
are the major elements of their speeches with respect to the
BANK codes as well as NLP, insider/outsider, emotion vs.
logic, etc.

Please note that each of these 4 speeches are readily available
from the internet and notations such as "(APPLAUSE)" were
part of the transcript I downloaded and are not my personal
commentary. In fact, I provide no commentary at all, as it is
up to you, Mr. and Mrs./Ms voter to make up your own mind
about the significance of each speech and how it impacts your
survival and higher level brain centers.   The order of the
speeches also is mostly in a B.A.N.(K.) order and doesn't
reflect my personal political preferences.

SENATOR TED CRUZ

Ted Cruz at a Christian University. Republican Presidential Candidate. Classified as Conservative Republican

Code Blue Speeches Ted Cruz

March 23, 2015

Here is a complete transcript of Ted Cruz's address at Liberty University in which he officially announced his 2016 presidential bid. From washingtonpost.com

CRUZ: Good to see you.

(APPLAUSE)

Thank you. (APPLAUSE)

Thank you so much, President Falwell. God bless Liberty University.

(APPLAUSE)

I am thrilled to join you today at the largest Christian university in the world.

(APPLAUSE)

Today I want to talk with you about the promise of America.

Imagine your parents when they were children. Imagine a little girl growing up in Wilmington, Delaware during World War II, the daughter of Irish and Italian Catholic family, working class. Her uncle ran numbers in Wilmington. She grew up with dozens of cousins because her mom was the second youngest of 17 kids. She had a difficult father, a man who drank far too much, and frankly didn't think that women should be educated.

And yet this young girl, pretty and shy, was driven, was bright, was inquisitive, and she became the first person in her family ever to go to college. In 1956, my mom, Eleanor, graduated from Rice University with a degree in math and became a pioneering computer programmer in the 1950s and 1960s.

(APPLAUSE)

Imagine a teenage boy, not much younger than many of you here today, growing up in Cuba. Jet black hair, skinny as a rail.

(LAUGHTER)

Involved in student council, and yet Cuba was not at a peaceful time. The dictator, Batista, was corrupt, he was oppressive. And this teenage boy joins a revolution. He joins a revolution against Batista, he begins fighting with other teenagers to free Cuba from the dictator. This boy at age 17 finds himself thrown in prison, finds himself tortured, beaten. And then at age 18, he flees Cuba, he comes to America.

Imagine for a second the hope that was in his heart as he rode that ferry boat across to Key West, and got on a Greyhound bus to head to Austin, Texas to begin working, washing dishes, making 50 cents an hour, coming to the one land on earth that has welcomed so many millions.

When my dad came to America in 1957, he could not have imagined what lay in store for him. Imagine a young married couple, living together in the 1970s, neither one of them has a personal relationship with Jesus. They have a little boy and they are both drinking far too much. They are living a fast life.

When I was three, my father decided to leave my mother and me. We were living in Calgary at the time, he got on a plane and he flew back to Texas, and he decided he didn't want to be married anymore and he didn't want to be a father to his 3-year-old son. And yet when he was in Houston, a friend, a colleague from the oil and gas business invited him to a Bible study, invited him to Clay Road (ph) Baptist Church, and there my father gave his life to Jesus Christ.

(APPLAUSE)

And God transformed his heart. And he drove to the airport, he bought a plane ticket, and he flew back to be with my mother and me.

(APPLAUSE)

There are people who wonder if faith is real. I can tell you, in my family there's not a second of doubt, because were it not for the transformative love of Jesus Christ, I would have been saved and I would have been raised by a single mom without my father in the household.

Imagine another little girl living in Africa, in Kenya and Nigeria. That's a diverse crowd.

(LAUGHTER)

Playing with kids, they spoke Swahili, she spoke English. Coming back to California.

(APPLAUSE)

Where her parents who had been missionaries in Africa raised her on the Central Coast. She starts a small business when she's in grade school baking bread. She calls it Heidi's Bakery. She and her brother compete baking bread. They bake thousands of loaves of bread and go to the local apple orchard where they sell the bread to people coming to pick apples. She goes on to a career in business, excelling and rising to the highest pinnacles, and then Heidi becomes my wife and my very best friend in the world.

(APPLAUSE)

Heidi becomes an incredible mom to our two precious little girls, Caroline and Catherine, the joys and loves of our life.

(APPLAUSE)

Imagine another teenage boy being raised in Houston, hearing stories from his dad about prison and torture in Cuba, hearing stories about how fragile liberty is, beginning to study the United States Constitution, learning about the incredible protections we have in this country that protect the God-given liberty of every American. Experiencing challenges at home.

In the 1980s, oil prices crater and his parents business go bankrupt. Heading off to school over a thousand miles away from home, in a place where he knew nobody, where he was alone and scared, and his parents going through bankruptcy meant there was no financial support at home, so at the age of 17, he went to get two jobs to help pay his way through school.

He took over $100,000 in school loans, loans I suspect a lot of ya'll can relate to, loans that I'll point out I just paid off a few years ago.

(APPLAUSE)

These are all of our stories. These are who we are as Americans.

And yet, for so many Americans, the promise of America seems more and more distant. What is the promise of America? The idea that -- the revolutionary idea that this country was founded upon, which is that our rights don't come from man. They come from God Almighty.

(APPLAUSE)

And that the purpose of the Constitution, as Thomas Jefferson put it, is to serve as chains to bind the mischief of government.

(APPLAUSE)

The incredible opportunity of the American dream, what has enabled millions of people from all over the world to come to America with nothing and to achieve anything. And then the American exceptionalism that has made this nation a clarion voice for freedom in the world, a shining city on a hill.

That's the promise of America. That is what makes this nation an indispensable nation, a unique nation in the history of the world.

And yet, so many fear that that promise is today unattainable. So many fear it is slipping away from our hands.

I want to talk to you this morning about reigniting the promise of America: 240 years ago on this very day, a 38-year-old lawyer named Patrick Henry...

(APPLAUSE)

... stood up just a hundred miles from here in Richmond, Virginia...

(APPLAUSE)

... and said, "Give me liberty or give me death."

(APPLAUSE) I want to ask each of you to imagine, imagine millions of courageous conservatives, all across America, rising up together to say in unison "we demand our liberty."

(APPLAUSE)

Today, roughly half of born again Christians aren't voting. They're staying home. Imagine instead millions of people of faith all across America coming out to the polls and voting our values.

(APPLAUSE)

Today millions of young people are scared, worried about the future, worried about what the future will hold. Imagine millions of young people coming together and standing together, saying "we will stand for liberty."

(APPLAUSE)

Think just how different the world would be. Imagine instead of economic stagnation, booming economic growth.

(APPLAUSE)

Instead of small businesses going out of business in record numbers, imagine small businesses growing and prospering. Imagine young people coming out of school with four, five, six job offers.

(APPLAUSE)

Imagine innovation thriving on the Internet as government regulators and tax collectors are kept at bay and more and more opportunity is created.

(APPLAUSE)

Imagine America finally becoming energy self-sufficient as millions and millions of high-paying jobs are created.

(APPLAUSE)

Five years ago today, the president signed Obamacare into law.

AUDIENCE: Boo.

Within hours, Liberty University went to court filing a lawsuit to stop that failed law.

(APPLAUSE)

Instead of the joblessness, instead of the millions forced into part-time work, instead of the millions who've lost their health insurance, lost their doctors, have faced skyrocketing health insurance premiums, imagine in 2017 a new president signing legislation repealing every word of Obamacare.

(APPLAUSE)

Imagine health care reform that keeps government out of the way between you and your doctor and that makes health insurance personal and portable and affordable.

(APPLAUSE)

Instead of a tax code that crushes innovation, that imposes burdens on families struggling to make ends met, imagine a simple flat tax...

(APPLAUSE)

... that lets every American fill out his or her taxes on a postcard.

(APPLAUSE)

Imagine abolishing the IRS.

(APPLAUSE)

Instead of the lawlessness and the president's unconstitutional executive amnesty, imagine a president that finally, finally, finally secures the borders.

(APPLAUSE)

And imagine a legal immigration system that welcomes and
celebrates those who come to achieve the American dream.

(APPLAUSE)

Instead of a federal government that wages an assault on our
religious liberty, that goes after Hobby Lobby, that goes after
the Little Sisters of the Poor, that goes after Liberty University,
imagine a federal government that stands for the First
Amendment rights of every American.

(APPLAUSE)

Instead of a federal government that works to undermine our
values, imagine a federal government that works to defend
the sanctity of human life...

(APPLAUSE)

... and to uphold the sacrament of marriage.

(APPLAUSE)

Instead of a government that works to undermine our Second
Amendment rights, that seeks to ban our ammunition...

(APPLAUSE)

... imagine a federal government that protects the right to keep
and bear arms of all law-abiding Americans.

(APPLAUSE)

Instead of a government that seizes your e-mails and your cell
phones, imagine a federal government that protected the
privacy rights of every American.

(APPLAUSE)

Instead of a federal government that seeks to dictate school
curriculum through Common Core...

(APPLAUSE)

... imagine repealing every word of Common Core.

(APPLAUSE)

Imagine embracing school choice as the civil rights issue of the next generation...

(APPLAUSE)

... that every single child, regardless of race, regardless of ethnicity, regardless of wealth or ZIP Code, every child in America has the right to a quality education.

(APPLAUSE)

And that's true from all of the above, whether is public schools, or charter schools, or private schools, or Christian schools, or parochial schools, or home schools, every child.

(APPLAUSE)

Instead of a president who boycotts Prime Minister Netanyahu, imagine a president who stands unapologetically with the nation of Israel.

(APPLAUSE)

Instead of a president who seeks to go to the United Nations to end-run Congress and the American people...

AUDIENCE MEMBER: That's horrible.

CRUZ: ... imagine a president who says "I will honor the Constitution, and under no circumstances will Iran be allowed to acquire a nuclear weapon."

(APPLAUSE)

Imagine a president who says "We will stand up and defeat radical Islamic terrorism..."

(APPLAUSE)

"... and we will call it by its name."

(APPLAUSE)

AUDIENCE MEMBER: That's right.

CRUZ: "We will defend the United States of America."

(APPLAUSE)

Now, all of these seem difficult, indeed to some they may seem unimaginable, and yet if you look in the history of our country, imagine it's 1775, and you and I were sitting there in Richmond listening to Patrick Henry say give me liberty or give me death.

Imagine its 1776 and we were watching the 54 signers of the Declaration of Independence stand together and pledge their lives, their fortunes, and their sacred honor to igniting the promise of America.

Imagine it was 1777 and we were watching General Washington as he lost battle, after battle, after battle in the freezing cold as his soldiers with no shoes were dying, fighting for freedom against the most powerful army in the world. That, too, seemed unimaginable.

Imagine its 1933 and we were listening to President Franklin Delano Roosevelt tell America at a time of crushing depression, at a time of a gathering storm abroad, that we have nothing to fear but fear itself.

Imagine it's 1979 and you and I were listening to Ronald Reagan.

(APPLAUSE)

And he was telling us that we would cut the top marginal tax rates from 70 percent all the way down to 28 percent, that we would go from crushing stagnation to booming economic growth, to millions being lifted out of poverty and into prosperity abundance. That the very day that he was sworn in, our hostages who were languishing in Iran would be released. And that within a decade we would win the Cold War and tear the Berlin Wall to the ground.

That would have seemed unimaginable, and yet, with the grace of God, that's exactly what happened.

(APPLAUSE)

From the dawn of this country, at every stage America has enjoyed God's providential blessing. Over and over again, when we face impossible odds, the American people rose to the challenge. You know, compared to that, repealing Obamacare and abolishing the IRS ain't all that tough.

(LAUGHTER)

The power of the American people when we rise up and stand for liberty knows no bounds.

(APPLAUSE)

If you're ready to join a grassroots army across this nation, coming together and standing for liberty, I'm going to ask you to break a rule here today and to take out your cell phones, and to text the word constitution to the number 33733. You can also text imagine. We're versatile.

Once again, text constitution to 33733. God's blessing has been on America from the very beginning of this nation, and I believe God isn't done with America yet.

(APPLAUSE)

I believe in you. I believe in the power of millions of courageous conservatives rising up to reignite the promise of America, and that is why today I am announcing that I'm running for president of the United States.

(APPLAUSE)

It is a time for truth. It is a time for liberty. It is a time to reclaim the Constitution of the United States.

(APPLAUSE)

I am honored to stand with each and every one of you courageous conservatives as we come together to reclaim the promise of America, to reclaim the mandate, the hope and opportunity for our children and our children's children. We stand together for liberty.

(APPLAUSE)

CRUZ: This is our fight. The answer will not come from Washington. It will come only from the men and women across this country, from men and women, from people of faith, from lovers of liberty, from people who respect the Constitution.

It will only come as it has come at every other time of challenge in this country, when the American people stand together and say we will get back to the principles that have made this country great. We will get back and restore that shining city on a hill that is the United States of America.

(APPLAUSE)

Thank you and God bless you.

SECRETARY HILLARY CLINTON

Hillary Clinton delivered the following remarks at the 2016 Democratic National Convention in Philadelphia.

Thank you. Thank you so much. Thank you. Thank you all so much. Thank you. Thank you. Thank you all very, very much. Thank you for that amazing welcome. Thank you all for the great convention that we've had.

And, Chelsea, thank you. I am so proud to be your mother and so proud of the woman you've become. Thank you for bringing Marc into our family and Charlotte and Aidan into the world. And, Bill, that conversation we started in the law library 45 years ago, it is still going strong.

That conversation has lasted through good times that filled us with joy and hard times that tested us. And I've even gotten a few words in along the way. On Tuesday night, I was so happy to see that my explainer-in-chief is still on the job. (Applause.) I'm also grateful to the rest of my family and to the friends of a lifetime.

For all of you whose hard work brought us here tonight and to those of you who joined this campaign this week, thank you. What a remarkable week it's been. We heard the man from Hope, Bill Clinton; and the man of hope, Barack Obama. America is stronger because of President Obama's leadership, and I am better because of his friendship.

We heard from our terrific Vice President, the one and only Joe Biden. He spoke from his big heart about our party's commitment to working people as only he can do.

And First Lady Michelle Obama reminded us that our children are watching and the president we elect is going to be their president, too.

And for those of you out there who are just getting to know Tim Kaine, you – you will soon understand why the people of Virginia keep promoting him from city council and mayor, to governor, and now Senator. And he will make our whole country proud as our vice president.
And I want to thank Bernie Sanders. Bernie. Bernie, your campaign inspired millions of Americans, particularly the young people who threw their hearts and souls into our primary. You put economic and social justice issues front and center, where they belong.

And to all of your supporters here and around the country, I want you to know I have heard you. Your cause is our cause. Our country needs your ideas, energy, and passion. That is the only way we can turn our progressive platform into real change for America. We wrote it together. Now let's go out and make it happen together.

My friends, we've come to Philadelphia, the birthplace of our nation, because what happened in this city 240 years ago still has something to teach us today. We all know the story, but we usually focus on how it turned out, and not enough on how close that story came to never being written at all. When representatives from 13 unruly colonies met just down the road from here, some wanted to stick with the king, and some wanted to stick it to the king.
The revolution hung in the balance. Then somehow they began listening to each other, compromising, finding common purpose. And by the time they left Philadelphia, they had begun to see themselves as one nation. That's what made it possible to stand up to a king. That took courage. They had courage. Our founders embraced the enduring truth that we are stronger together.

Now America is once again at a moment of reckoning. Powerful forces are threatening to pull us apart. Bonds of trust and respect are fraying. And just as with our founders, there are no guarantees. It truly is up to us. We have to decide whether we will all work together so we can all rise together. Our country's motto is e pluribus unum: out of many, we are one. Will we stay true to that motto?

Well, we heard Donald Trump's answer last week at his convention. He wants to divide us from the rest of the world and from each other. He's betting that the perils of today's world will blind us to its unlimited promise. He's taken the Republican Party a long way from "Morning in America" to "Midnight in America." He wants us to fear the future and fear each other.

Well, a great Democratic President, Franklin Delano
Roosevelt, came up with the perfect rebuke to Trump more
than eighty years ago, during a much more perilous time: "The
only thing we have to fear is fear itself."

Now we are clear-eyed about what our country is up against,
but we are not afraid. We will rise to the challenge, just as we
always have. We will not build a wall. Instead, we will build an
economy where everyone who wants a good job can get one.
And we'll build a path to citizenship for millions of immigrants
who are already contributing to our economy. We will not ban
a religion. We will work with all Americans and our allies to
fight and defeat terrorism.

Yet, we know there is a lot to do. Too many people haven't had
a pay raise since the crash. There's too much inequality, too
little social mobility, too much paralysis in Washington, too
many threats at home and abroad.

But just look for a minute at the strengths we bring as
Americans to meet these challenges. We have the most
dynamic and diverse people in the world. We have the most
tolerant and generous young people we've ever had. We have
the most powerful military, the most innovative
entrepreneurs, the most enduring values – freedom and
equality, justice and opportunity. We should be so proud that
those words are associated with us. I have to tell you, as your
Secretary of State, I went to 112 countries. When people hear
those words, they hear America.

So don't let anyone tell you that our country is weak. We're not. Don't let anyone tell you we don't have what it takes. We do. And most of all, don't believe anyone who says, "I alone can fix it." Yes. Those were actually Donald Trump's words in Cleveland. And they should set off alarm bells for all of us. Really? "I alone can fix it? Isn't he forgetting troops on the front lines, police officers and firefighters who run toward danger, doctors and nurses who care for us? Teachers who change lives, entrepreneurs who see possibilities in every problem, mothers who lost children to violence and are building a movement to keep other kids safe? He's forgetting every last one of us. Americans don't say, "I alone fix can it." We say, "We'll fix it together."

And remember. Remember. Our founders fought a revolution and wrote a Constitution so America would never be a nation where one person had all the power. 240 years later, we still put our faith in each other. Look at what happened in Dallas. After the assassinations of five brave police officers, Police Chief David Brown asked the community to support his force, maybe even join them. And do you know how the community responded? Nearly 500 people applied in just 12 days.

That's how Americans answer when the call for help goes out. 20 years ago, I wrote a book called It Takes a Village. And a lot of people looked at the title and asked, what the heck do you mean by that? This is what I mean. None of us can raise a family, build a business, heal a community, or lift a country totally alone. America needs every one of us to lend our energy, our talents, our ambition to making our nation better and stronger. I believe that with all my heart. That's why "Stronger Together" is not just a lesson from our history, it's not just a slogan for our campaign, it's a guiding principle for the country we've always been, and the future we're going to build.

A country where the economy works for everyone, not just those at the top. Where you can get a good job and send your kids to a good school no matter what ZIP Code you live in. A country where all our children can dream, and those dreams are within reach. Where families are strong, communities are safe, and, yes, where love trumps hate. That's the country we're fighting for. That's the future we're working toward. And so, my friends, it is with humility, determination, and boundless confidence in America's promise that I accept your nomination for president of the United States.

Now, sometimes the people at this podium are new to the national stage. As you know, I'm not one of those people. I've been your first lady, served eight years as a senator from the great state of New York. Then I represented all of you as Secretary of State. But my job titles only tell you what I've done. They don't tell you why. The truth is, through all these years of public service, the service part has always come easier to me than the public part. I get it that some people just don't know what to make of me. So let me tell you.

The family I'm from, well, no one had their name on big buildings. My families were builders of a different kind, builders in the way most American families are. They used whatever tools they had, whatever God gave them, and whatever life in America provided, and built better lives and better futures for their kids.

My grandfather worked in the same Scranton lace mill for 50 years because he believed that if he gave everything he had, his children would have a better life than he did. And he was right. My dad, Hugh, made it to college. He played football at Penn State and enlisted in the Navy after Pearl Harbor. When the war was over he started his own small business, printing fabric for draperies. I remember watching him stand for hours over silkscreens. He wanted to give my brothers and me opportunities he never had, and he did.

My mother, Dorothy, was abandoned by her parents as a
young girl. She ended up on her own at 14, working as a
housemaid. She was saved by the kindness of others. Her first
grade teacher saw she had nothing to eat at lunch, and brought
extra food to share the entire year. The lesson she passed on to
me years later stuck with me: No one gets through life alone.
We have to look out for each other and lift each other up. And
she made sure I learned the words from our Methodist faith:
"Do all the good you can, for all the people you can, in all the
ways you can, as long as ever you can."

So I went to work for the Children's Defense Fund, going door
to door in New Bedford, Massachusetts on behalf of children
with disabilities who were denied the chance to go to school.
Remember meeting a young girl in a wheelchair on the small
back porch of her house. She told me how badly she wanted to
go to school. It just didn't seem possible in those days. And I
couldn't stop thinking of my mother and what she'd gone
through as a child. It became clear to me that simply caring is
not enough. To drive real progress, you have to change both
hearts and laws. You need both understanding and action.

So we gathered facts. We build a coalition. And our work
helped convince Congress to ensure access to education for all
students with disabilities. It's a big idea, isn't it? Every kid
with a disability has the right to go to school. But how do you
make an idea like that real? You do it step by step, year by
year, sometimes even door by door. My heart just swelled
when I saw Anastasia Somoza representing millions of young
people on this stage because we changed our law to make sure
she got an education.

So it's true. I sweat the details of policy, whether we're talking about the exact level of lead in the drinking water in Flint, Michigan the number of mental health facilities in Iowa, or the cost of your prescription drugs. Because it's not just a detail if it's your kid, if it's your family. It's a big deal. And it should be a big deal to your president, too.

After the four days of this convention, you've seen some of the people who've inspired me, people who let me into their lives and became a part of mine, people like Ryan Moore and Lauren Manning. They told their stories Tuesday night. I first met Ryan as a 7-year-old. He was wearing a full body brace that must have weighed 40 pounds because I leaned over to lift him up. Children like Ryan kept me going when our plan for universal health care failed, and kept me working with leaders of both parties to help create the Children's Health Insurance Program that covers eight million kids in our country. Lauren Manning, who stood here with such grace and power, was gravely injured on 9/11.

It was the thought of her, and Debbie Stage. John who you saw in the movie, and John Dolan and Joe Sweeney and all the victims and survivors, that kept me working as hard as I could in the Senate on behalf of 9/11 families and our first responders who got sick from their time at Ground Zero. I was thinking of Lauren, Debbie, and all the others ten years later in the White House Situation Room, when President Obama made the courageous decision that finally brought Osama bin Laden to justice.

And in this campaign I've met many more people who motivate me to keep fighting for change, and with your help, I will carry all of your voices and stories with me to the White House. And you heard from Republicans and Independents who are supporting our campaign. Well, I will be a president for Democrats, Republicans, Independents, for the struggling, the striving, the successful, for all those who vote for me and for those who don't. For all Americans together.

Tonight, we've reached a milestone in our nation's march toward a more perfect union: the first time that a major party has nominated a woman for president. Standing here as my mother's daughter, and my daughter's mother, I'm so happy this day has come. I'm happy for grandmothers and little girls and everyone in between. I'm happy for boys and men – because when any barrier falls in America, it clears the way for everyone. After all, when there are no ceilings, the sky's the limit. So let's keep going until every one of the 161 million women and girls across America has the opportunity she deserves to have. But even more important than the history we make tonight is the history we will write together in the years ahead. Let's begin with what we're going to do to help working people in our country get ahead and stay ahead.

Now, I don't think President Obama and Vice President Biden get the credit they deserve for saving us from the worst economic crisis of our lifetimes. Our economy is so much stronger than when they took office. Nearly 15 million new private sector jobs. Twenty million more Americans with health insurance. And an auto industry that just had its best year ever.

Now, that's real progress. But none of us can be satisfied with the status quo. Not by a long shot. We're still facing deep-seated problems that developed long before the recession and have stayed with us through the recovery. I've gone around the country talking to working families. And I've heard from many who feel like the economy sure isn't working for them. Some of you are frustrated – even furious. And you know what? You're right. It's not yet working the way it should.

Americans are willing to work – and work hard. But right now, an awful lot of people feel there is less and less respect for the work they do. And less respect for them, period. Democrats, we are the party of working people. But we haven't done a good enough job showing we get what you're going through, and we're going to do something to help.

So tonight I want to tell you how we will empower Americans to live better lives. My primary mission as president will be to create more opportunity and more good jobs with rising wages right here in the United States. From my first day in office to my last. Especially in places that for too long have been left out and left behind. From our inner cities to our small towns, from Indian country to coal country. From communities ravaged by addiction to regions hollowed out by plant closures.

And here's what I believe. I believe America thrives when the middle class thrives. I believe our economy isn't working the way it should because our democracy isn't working the way it should. That's why we need to appoint Supreme Court justices who will get money out of politics and expand voting rights, not restrict them. And if necessary, we will pass a constitutional amendment to overturn Citizens United.

I believe American corporations that have gotten so much from our country should be just as patriotic in return. Many of them are, but too many aren't. It's wrong to take tax breaks with one hand and give out pink slips with the other. And I believe Wall Street can never, ever be allowed to wreck Main Street again.

And I believe in science. I believe that climate change is real and that we can save our planet while creating millions of good-paying clean energy jobs.

I believe that when we have millions of hardworking immigrants contributing to our economy, it would be self-defeating and inhumane to try to kick them out. Comprehensive immigration reform will grow our economy and keep families together – and it's the right thing to do. So whatever party you belong to, or if you belong to no party at all, if you share these beliefs, this is your campaign.

If you believe that companies should share profits, not pad executive bonuses, join us. If you believe the minimum wage should be a living wage, and no one working full-time should have to raise their children in poverty, join us.
If you believe that every man, woman, and child in America has the right to affordable health care, join us! If you believe that we should say no to unfair trade deals; that we should stand up to China; that we should support our steelworkers and autoworkers and homegrown manufacturers, then join us.

If you believe we should expand Social Security and protect a woman's right to make her own heath care decisions, then join us. And yes, yes, if you believe that your working mother, wife, sister, or daughter deserves equal pay join us. That's how we're going to make sure this economy works for everyone, not just those at the top.

Now, you didn't hear any of this, did you, from Donald Trump at his convention. He spoke for 70-odd minutes – and I do mean odd. And he offered zero solutions. But we already know he doesn't believe these things. No wonder he doesn't like talking about his plans. You might have noticed, I love talking about mine.

In my first 100 days, we will work with both parties to pass the biggest investment in new, good-paying jobs since World War II. Jobs in manufacturing, clean energy, technology and innovation, small business, and infrastructure. If we invest in infrastructure now, we'll not only create jobs today, but lay the foundation for the jobs of the future.

And we will also transform the way we prepare our young people for those jobs. Bernie Sanders and I will work together to make college tuition-free for the middle class and debt-free for all. We will also – we will also liberate millions of people who already have student debt. It's just not right that Donald Trump can ignore his debts, and students and families can't refinance their debts.

And something we don't say often enough: Sure, college is crucial, but a four-year degree should not be the only path to a good job. We will help more people learn a skill or practice a trade and make a good living doing it. We will give small businesses, like my dad's, a boost, make it easier to get credit. Way too many dreams die in the parking lots of banks. In America, if you can dream it, you should be able to build it.

And we will help you balance family and work. And you know what, if fighting for affordable child care and paid family leave is playing the "woman card," then deal me in.

Now – now, here's the other thing. Now, we're not only going to make all of these investments. We're going to pay for every single one of them. And here's how. Wall Street, corporations, and the super-rich are going to start paying their fair share of taxes. This is – this is not because we resent success, but when more than 90 percent of the gains have gone to the top 1 percent, that's where the money is. And we are going to follow the money. And if companies take tax breaks and then ship jobs overseas, we'll make them pay us back. And we'll put that money to work where it belongs: creating jobs here at home.

Now, I imagine that some of you are sitting at home thinking, well, that all sounds pretty good, but how are you going to get it done? How are you going to break through the gridlock in Washington? Well, look at my record. I've worked across the aisle to pass laws and treaties and to launch new programs that help millions of people. And if you give me the chance, that's exactly what I'll do as President.

But then – but then I also imagine people are thinking out there, but Trump, he's a businessman. He must know something about the economy. Well, let's take a closer look, shall we? In Atlantic City, 60 miles from here, you will find contractors and small businesses who lost everything because Donald Trump refused to pay his bills. Now, remember what the President said last night. Don't boo. Vote.

But think of this. People who did the work and needed the money, not because he couldn't pay them, but because he wouldn't pay them, he just stiffed them. And you know that sales pitch he's making to be president: put your faith in him, and you'll win big? That's the same sales pitch he made to all those small businesses. Then Trump walked away and left working people holding the bag.

He also talks a big game about putting America first. Well, please explain what part of America First leads him to make Trump ties in China, not Colorado; Trump suits in Mexico, not Michigan; Trump furniture in Turkey, not Ohio; Trump picture frames in India, not Wisconsin.Donald Trump says he wants to make America great again. Well, he could start by actually making things in America again.

Now, the choice we face in this election is just as stark when it comes to our national security.

Anyone – anyone reading the news can see the threats and turbulence we face. From Baghdad and Kabul, to Nice and Paris and Brussels, from San Bernardino to Orlando, we're dealing with determined enemies that must be defeated. So it's no wonder that people are anxious and looking for reassurance, looking for steady leadership, wanting a leader who understands we are stronger when we work with our allies around the world and care for our veterans here at home. Keeping our nation safe and honoring the people who do that work will be my highest priority.

I'm proud that we put a lid on Iran's nuclear program without firing a single shot. Now we have to enforce it, and we must keep supporting Israel's security. I'm proud that we shaped a global climate agreement. Now we have to hold every country accountable to their commitments, including ourselves. And I'm proud to stand by our allies in NATO against any threat they face, including from Russia.

I've laid out my strategy for defeating ISIS. We will strike their sanctuaries from the air and support local forces taking them out on the ground. We will surge our intelligence so we detect and prevent attacks before they happen. We will disrupt their efforts online to reach and radicalize young people in our country. It won't be easy or quick, but make no mistake we will prevail.

Now Donald Trump – Donald Trump says, and this is a quote, "I know more about ISIS than the generals do." No, Donald, you don't.

He thinks – he thinks he knows more than our military because he claimed our armed forces are "a disaster." Well, I've had the privilege to work closely with our troops and our veterans for many years, including as a Senator on the Armed Services Committee. And I know how wrong he is. Our military is a national treasure. We entrust our commander-in-chief to make the hardest decisions our nation faces: decisions about war and peace, life and death. A president should respect the men and women who risk their lives to serve our country, including – including Captain Khan and the sons of Tim Kaine and Mike Pence, both Marines. So just ask yourself: Do you really think Donald Trump has the temperament to be commander-in-chief? Donald Trump can't even handle the rough-and-tumble of a presidential campaign. He loses his cool at the slightest provocation – when he's gotten a tough question from a reporter, when he's challenged in a debate, when he sees a protestor at a rally. Imagine, if you dare imagine, imagine him in the Oval Office facing a real crisis. A man you can bait with a tweet is not a man we can trust with nuclear weapons.

I can't put it any better than Jackie Kennedy did after the Cuban Missile Crisis. She said that what worried President Kennedy during that very dangerous time was that a war might be started – not by big men with self-control and restraint, but by little men, the ones moved by fear and pride.

America's strength doesn't come from lashing out. It relies on smarts, judgment, cool resolve, and the precise and strategic application of power. And that's the kind of commander-in-chief I pledge to be.

And if we're serious about keeping our country safe, we also can't afford to have a president who's in the pocket of the gun lobby. I'm not here to repeal the Second Amendment. I'm not here to take away your guns. I just don't want you to be shot by someone who shouldn't have a gun in the first place.

We will work tirelessly with responsible gun owners to pass common-sense reforms and keep guns out of the hands of criminals, terrorists, and all others who would do us harm. For decades, people have said this issue was too hard to solve and the politics too hot to touch. But I ask you: How can we just stand by and do nothing? You heard, you saw, family members of people killed by gun violence on this stage. You heard, you saw family members of police officers killed in the line of duty because they were outgunned by criminals. I refuse to believe we can't find common ground here. We have to heal the divides in our country, not just on guns but on race, immigration, and more.

And that starts with listening, listening to each other, trying as best we can to walk in each other's shoes. So let's put ourselves in the shoes of young black and Latino men and women who face the effects of systemic racism and are made to feel like their lives are disposable. Let's put ourselves in the shoes of police officers, kissing their kids and spouses goodbye every day and heading off to do a dangerous and necessary job. We will reform our criminal justice system from end to end, and rebuild trust between law enforcement and the communities they serve. And we will defend – we will defend all our rights: civil rights, human rights, and voting rights; women's rights and workers' rights; LGBT rights and the rights of people with disabilities. And we will stand up against mean and divisive rhetoric wherever it comes from.

For the past year, many people made the mistake of laughing off Donald Trump's comments, excusing him as an entertainer just putting on a show. They thought he couldn't possibly mean all the horrible things he says, like when he called women "pigs" or said that an American judge couldn't be fair because of his Mexican heritage, or when he mocks and mimics a reporter with a disability, or insults prisoners of war – like John McCain, a hero and a patriot who deserves our respect.

Now, at first, I admit, I couldn't believe he meant it, either. It was just too hard to fathom, that someone who wants to lead our nation could say those things, could be like that. But here's the sad truth: There is no other Donald Trump. This is it. And in the end, it comes down to what Donald Trump doesn't get: America is great because America is good.

So enough with the bigotry and the bombast. Donald Trump's not offering real change. He's offering empty promises. And what are we offering? A bold agenda to improve the lives of people across our country – to keep you safe, to get you good jobs, to give your kids the opportunities they deserve.

The choice is clear, my friends. Every generation of Americans has come together to make our country freer, fairer, and stronger. None of us ever have or can do it alone. I know that at a time when so much seems to be pulling us apart, it can be hard to imagine how we'll ever pull together. But I'm here to tell you tonight – progress is possible. I know. I know because I've seen it in the lives of people across America who get knocked down and get right back up.

And I know it from my own life. More than a few times, I've had to pick myself up and get back in the game. Like so much else in my life, I got this from my mother too. She never let me back down from any challenge. When I tried to hide from a neighborhood bully, she literally blocked the door. "Go back out there," she said. And she was right. You have to stand up to bullies. You have to keep working to make things better, even when the odds are long and the opposition is fierce.

We lost our mother a few years ago, but I miss her every day. And I still hear her voice urging me to keep working, keep fighting for right, no matter what. That's what we need to do together as a nation. And though "we may not live to see the glory," as the song from the musical Hamilton goes, "let us gladly join the fight." Let our legacy be about "planting seeds in a garden you never get to see."

That's why we're here, not just in this hall, but on this Earth. The Founders showed us that, and so have many others since. They were drawn together by love of country, and the selfless passion to build something better for all who follow. That is the story of America. And we begin a new chapter tonight.

Yes, the world is watching what we do. Yes, America's destiny is ours to choose. So let's be stronger together, my fellow Americans. Let's look to the future with courage and confidence. Let's build a better tomorrow for our beloved children and our beloved country. And when we do, America will be greater than ever.

Thank you and may God bless you and the United States of America.

DONALD TRUMP

Donald Trump Presidential Nomination Acceptance Speech at Republican Convention

NOTE: Highlighted areas are fact checks by NPR staff. Their notes available online at the source of this transcript.
http://www.npr.org/2016/07/21/486883610/fact-check-donald-trumps-republican-convention-speech-annotated

Thank you, thank you. Thank you very much.

Friends, delegates and fellow Americans: I humbly and gratefully accept your nomination for the presidency of the United States.

USA, USA, USA, USA, USA.

Who would have believed that when we started this journey // because we are a team would have received almost 14 million votes the most in the history of the Republican party and that the Republican party would get 60 percent more votes than it received eight years ago. Who would have believed this. Who would have believed this.

The Democrats on the other hand received 20 percent fewer votes than they got four years ago. Not so good. Not so good.

Together, we will lead our party back to the White House, and we will lead our country back to safety, prosperity, and peace.

We will be a country of generosity and warmth.

But we will also be a country of law and order.

Our Convention occurs at a moment of crisis for our nation.
The attacks on our police, and the terrorism *of* our cities,
threaten our very way of life. Any politician who does not
grasp this danger is not fit to lead our country.
Americans watching this address tonight have seen the recent
images of violence in our streets and the chaos in our
communities. Many have witnessed this violence personally,
some have even been its victims. I have a message for all of
you: the crime and violence that today afflicts our nation will
soon, *and I mean very soon,* come to an end.
Beginning on January 20th *of* 2017, safety will be restored.

The most basic duty of government is to defend the lives of its
own citizens. Any government that fails to do so is a
government unworthy to lead. It is finally time for a
straightforward assessment of the state of our nation.

I will present the facts plainly and honestly.

We cannot afford to be so politically correct anymore.

So if you want to hear the corporate spin, the carefully-crafted
lies, and the media myths the Democrats are holding their
convention next week. *Go there.*
But here, at our convention, there will be no lies. We will
honor the American people with the truth, and nothing else.

These are the facts: Decades of progress made in bringing
down crime are now being reversed by this Administration's
rollback of criminal enforcement.Homicides last year
increased by 17 percent in America's fifty largest cities. That's
the largest increase in 25 years.

In our nation's capital, killings have risen by 50 percent. They are up nearly 60% in nearby Baltimore.

In the President's hometown of Chicago, more than 2,000 people have been the victims of shootings this year alone.

And more than 4,000 have been killed in the Chicago area since he took office.
The number of police officers killed in the line of duty has risen by almost 50% compared to this point last year.

Nearly 180,000 illegal immigrants with criminal records, ordered deported from our country, are tonight roaming free to threaten peaceful citizens.

The number of new illegal immigrant families who have crossed the border so far this year already exceeds the entire total from 2015.

They are being released by the tens of thousands into our communities with no regard for the impact on public safety or resources.

One such border-crosser was released and made his way to Nebraska. There, he ended the life of an innocent young girl named Sarah Root. She was 21 years-old, and was killed the day after graduating from college with a 4.0 Grade Point Average. Number one in her class. Her killer was then released a second time, and he is now a fugitive from the law. I've met Sarah's beautiful family. But to this Administration, their amazing daughter was just one more American life that wasn't worth protecting. No more.

One more child to sacrifice on the order and on the altar of open borders.

What about our economy? Again, I will tell you the plain facts that have been edited out of your nightly news and your morning newspaper: Nearly 4 in 10 African-American children are living in poverty, while 58% of African-American youth are *now* not employed.

2 million more Latinos are in poverty today than when President *Obama* took his oath of office less than eight years ago.

Another 14 million people have left the workforce entirely.

Household incomes are down more than $4,000 since the year 2000. *That's sixteen years ago.*

Our trade deficit has reached an all-time high think of this, think of this, our trade deficit is nearly $800 billion, think of that, 800 billion dollars, last year alone. We're going to fix that.

The budget is no better. President Obama has almost doubled our national debt to more than $19 trillion, and growing. And yet, what do we have to show for it? Our roads and bridges are falling apart, our airports are Third World condition, and forty-three million Americans are on food stamps.

Now let us consider the state of affairs abroad. Not only have our citizens endured domestic disaster, but they've lived through one international humiliation after another.One after another. We all remember the images of our sailors being forced to their knees by their Iranian captors at gunpoint.This was just prior to the signing of the Iran deal, which gave back to Iran $150 billion and gave us *absolutely* nothing – it will go down in history as one of the worst deals ever *negotiated*.

Another humiliation came when president Obama drew a red line in Syria – and the whole world knew it meant *absolutely* nothing. In Libya, our consulate – the symbol of American prestige around the globe – was brought down in flames.

America is far less safe – and the world is far less stable – than when Obama made the decision to put Hillary Clinton in charge of America's foreign policy.

[Editor's note: Crowd chants "Lock her up."]

Let's defeat her in November, okay?

I am certain that it was a decision that President Obama truly regrets.

Her bad instincts and her bad judgment – something pointed out by Bernie Sanders – are what caused so many of the disasters unfolding today. Let's review the record.

In 2009, pre-Hillary, ISIS was not even on the map. Libya was stable. Egypt was peaceful. Iraq was seeing and really a big big reduction in violence. Iran was being choked by sanctions. Syria was somewhat under control. After four years of Hillary Clinton, what do we have? ISIS has spread across the region, and the entire world. Libya is in ruins, and our Ambassador and his staff were left helpless to die at the hands of savage killers. Egypt was turned over to the radical Muslim brotherhood, forcing the military to retake control. Iraq is in chaos. Iran is on the path to nuclear weapons. Syria is engulfed in a civil war and a refugee crisis, now threatens the West. After fifteen years of wars in the Middle East, after trillions of dollars spent and thousands of lives lost, the situation is worse than it has ever been before. This is the legacy of Hillary Clinton: death, destruction, terrorism, and weakness. But Hillary Clinton's legacy does not have to be America's legacy.

The problems we face now – poverty and violence at home, war and destruction abroad – will last only as long as we continue relying on the same politicians who created them in the first place.

A change in leadership is required to *produce a change in* outcomes.

Tonight, I will share with you my plan *for* action for America. The most important difference between our plan and that of our opponents, is that our plan will put America First. Americanism, not globalism, will be our credo. As long as we are led by politicians who will not put America First, then we can be assured that other nations will not treat America with respect. *The respect that we deserve.*

The American People will come first once again.

My plan will begin with safety at home – which means safe neighborhoods, secure borders, and protection from terrorism. There can be no prosperity without law and order.

On the economy, I will outline reforms to add millions of new jobs and trillions in new wealth that can be used to rebuild America.

A number of these reforms that I will outline tonight will be opposed by some of our nation's most powerful special interests. That's because these interests have rigged our political and economic system for their exclusive benefit. Believe me. It's for their benefit.

Big business, elite media and major donors are lining up behind the campaign of my opponent because they know she will keep our rigged system in place.

They are throwing money at her because they have total control over everything single thing she does. She is their puppet, and they pull the strings.

That is why Hillary Clinton's message is that things will never change. Never ever.

My message is that things have to change – and they have to change right now.

Every day I wake up determined to deliver a better life for the people all across this nation that have been neglected, ignored, and abandoned. I have visited the laid-off factory workers, and the communities crushed by our horrible and unfair trade deals. These are the forgotten men and women of our country. And they are forgotten. But they're not going to be forgotten long.

These are people who work hard but no longer have a voice. I am your voice.

I have embraced crying mothers who have lost their children because our politicians put their personal agendas before the national good. I have no patience for injustice -

[Editor's note: Protester interrupts, crowd shouts "USA"]
How great are our police! And how great is Cleveland?

Thank you.

I have no patience for injustice. No tolerance for government incompetence of which there is so much, no sympathy for leaders who fail their citizens. When innocent people suffer, because our political system lacks the will, or the courage, or the basic decency to enforce our laws – or still worse, has sold out to some corporate lobbyist for cash – I am not able to look the other way. And I won't look the other way.

And when a Secretary of State illegally stores her emails on a private server, deletes 33,000 of them so the authorities can't see her crime, puts our country at risk, lies about it in every different form and faces no consequence – I know that corruption has reached a level like never *ever* before *in our country.*

When the FBI Director says that the Secretary of State was "extremely careless" and "negligent," in handling our classified secrets, I also know that these terms are minor compared to what she actually did.

They were just used to save her from facing justice for her terrible, terrible crimes.

In fact, her single greatest accomplishment may be committing such egregious crime and getting away with it – especially when others who have done far less, have paid so dearly. When that same Secretary of State rakes in millions and millions of dollars trading access and favors to special interests and foreign powers I know the time for action has come.

I have joined the political arena so that the powerful can no longer beat up on people *who* cannot defend themselves. Nobody knows the system better than me.

Which is why I alone can fix it.

I have seen firsthand how the system is rigged against our citizens, just like it was rigged against Bernie Sanders – he never had a chance. Never had a chance. But his supporters will join our movement, because we will fix his biggest *single* issue: trade *deals that strip our country of its jobs and strip us of our wealth as a country.*

Millions of Democrats will join our movement, because we are going to fix the system so it works fairly and justly for all Americans.

In this cause, I am proud to have at my side the next Vice President of the United States: Governor Mike Pence of Indiana. And a great guy.

We will bring the same economic success to America that Mike brought to Indiana. Which is amazing.

He's a man of character and accomplishment. He's the man for the job.

The first task for our new Administration will be to liberate our citizens from the crime and terrorism and lawlessness that threatens our community. America was shocked to its core when our police officers in Dallas were so brutally executed. Immediately after Dallas, we have seen continued threats and violence against our law enforcement officials. Law officers have been shot or killed in recent days in Georgia, Missouri, Wisconsin, Kansas, Michigan and Tennessee.

On Sunday, more police were gunned down in Baton Rouge, Louisiana. Three were killed, and three were very, very badly injured. An attack on law enforcement is an attack on all Americans.

I have a message to every last person threatening the peace on our streets and the safety of our police: when I take the oath of office next year, I will restore law and order to our country. Believe me. Believe me.
I will work with, and appoint, the best and brightest prosecutors and law enforcement officials to get the job properly done.

In this race for the White House, I am the Law And Order candidate.

The irresponsible rhetoric of our President, who has used the pulpit of the presidency to divide us by race and color, has made America a more dangerous environment that frankly that I have ever seen of anybody in this room has ever watched or seen.

This Administration has failed America's inner cities. Remember, it has failed America's inner cities. It's failed them on education. It's failed them on jobs. It's failed them on crime. It's failed them in every way and at every single level. When I am President, I will work to ensure that all of our kids are treated equally, and protected equally.

Every action I take, I will ask myself: does this make better for young Americans in Baltimore, in Chicago, in Detroit, in Ferguson who have really, in every way folks, the same right to live out their dreams as any other child in America? Any other child.

To make life safe for all of our citizens, we must also address the growing threats from outside the country. We are going to defeat the barbarians of ISIS and we're going to defeat them fast.

Once again, France is the victim of brutal Islamic terrorism. Men, women and children viciously mowed down. Lives ruined. Families ripped apart. A nation in mourning. The damage and devastation that can be inflicted by Islamic radicals has been proven over and over – at the World Trade Center, at an office party in San Bernardino, at the Boston Marathon, at a military recruiting center in Chattanooga, Tennessee. And many many other locations.

Only weeks ago, in Orlando, Florida, 49 wonderful Americans were savagely murdered by an Islamic terrorist. This time, the terrorist targeted LGBTQ community. No good, and we're going to stop it.

As your President, I will do everything in my power to protect our LGBTQ citizens from the violence and oppression of a hateful foreign ideology. *Believe me.*

And I have to say as a Republican it is so nice to hear you cheering for what I just said. Thank you.

To protect us from terrorism, we need to focus on three things. We must have the best, absolutely the best gathering of intelligence anywhere in the world. The best. We must abandon the failed policy of nation building and regime change that Hillary Clinton pushed in Iraq, in Libya, in Egypt and in Syria. Instead, we must work with all of our allies who share our goal of destroying ISIS and stamping out Islamic terrorism and doing it now, doing it quickly. We're going to win. We're going to win fast.

This includes working with our greatest ally in the region, the State of Israel.

Recently, I have said NATO is obsolete because it did not properly cover terror. And also that many of the member countries were not paying their fair share. As usual, the United States has been picking up the costs. Shortly thereafter, it was announced that NATO will be setting up a new program in order to combat terrorism. A true step in the right direction.

Lastly, and very importantly, we must immediately suspend immigration from any nation that has been compromised by terrorism until such time as proven vetting mechanisms have been put in place. We don't want them in our country.

My opponent has called for a radical 550% increase in Syrian, think of this. Think of this, this is not believable but this is what's happening. A 550 percent increase in Syrian refugees on top of existing massive refugee flows coming into our country already under the leadership of President Obama. She proposes this despite the fact that there's no way to screen these refugees in order to find out who they are or where they come from.

I only want to admit individuals into our country who will support our values and love our people.

Anyone who endorses violence, hatred or oppression is not welcome in our country and never *ever* will be.
Decades of record immigration have produced lower wages and higher unemployment for our citizens, especially for African-American and Latino workers. We are going to have an immigration system that works, but one that works for the American people.

On Monday, we heard from three parents whose children
were killed by illegal immigrants: Mary Ann Mendoza, Sabine
Durden, and my friend Jamiel Shaw. They are just three brave
representatives of many thousands who have suffered so
greatly. Of all my travels in this country, nothing has affected
me more, nothing even close I have to tell you, than the time I
have spent with the mothers and fathers who have lost their
children to violence spilling across our borders which we can
solve. We have to solve it.

These families have no special interests to represent them.
There are no demonstrators to protect them and certainly
none to protest on their behalf. My opponent will never meet
with them, or share in their pain. Believe me. Instead, my
opponent wants Sanctuary Cities.

But where was the sanctuary for Kate Steinle?

Where was the Sanctuary for the children of Mary Ann, and
Sabine and Jamiel? Where was sanctuary for all the other, it's
so sad to even be talking about it, because we can solve this
problem so quickly. Where was the sanctuary for all of the
Americans who have been so brutally murdered, and who
have suffered so horribly? These wounded American families
have been alone. But they are not alone any longer.

Tonight, this candidate and *the* whole nation stand in their
corner to support them, to send them our love, and to pledge
in their honor that we will save countless more families from
suffering *and* the same awful fate.
We are going to build a great border wall to stop illegal
immigration, to stop the gangs and the violence, and to stop
the drugs from pouring into our communities.

I have been honored to receive the endorsement of America's Border Patrol Agents.

And will work directly with them to protect the integrity of our lawful, lawful, lawful immigration system. Lawful.

By ending catch-and-release on the border, we will end the cycle of human smuggling and violence. Illegal border crossings will go down. We will stop it, it won't be happening very much anymore. Believe me.

Peace will be restored. By enforcing the rules for millions who overstay their visas, our laws will finally receive the respect that they deserve.

Tonight, I want every American whose demands for immigration security have been denied – and every politician who has denied them – to listen very, very closely to the words I am about to say. On January 20th of 2017, the day I take the oath of office, Americans will finally wake up in a country where the laws of the United States are enforced.

We are going to be considerate and compassionate to everyone. But my greatest compassion will be for our own struggling citizens.

USA. USA. USA.
[Editor's note: Trump chanted along with the crowd here.]
My plan is the exact opposite of the radical and dangerous immigration policy of Hillary Clinton. Americans want relief from uncontrolled immigration. Which is what we have now. Communities want relief. Yet Hillary Clinton is proposing mass amnesty, mass immigration, and mass lawlessness.

Her plan will overwhelm your schools and hospitals, further reduce your jobs and wages, and make it harder for recent immigrants to escape the tremendous cycle poverty that they're going through right now and make it almost impossible for them to join the middle class.

I have a different vision for our workers. It begins with a new, fair trade policy that protects our jobs and stands up to countries that cheat. Of which there are many.

It's been a signature message of my campaign from day one, and it will be a signature feature of my presidency from the moment I take the oath of office.

I have made billions of dollars in business making deals – now I'm going to make our country rich again.

Using the greatest business people in the world, which our country has, I am going to turn our bad trade agreements into great trade agreements.

America has lost nearly-one third of its manufacturing jobs since 1997, following the enactment of disastrous trade deals supported by Bill and Hillary Clinton. Remember, it was Bill Clinton who signed NAFTA, one of the worst economic deals ever made by our country. Or frankly, any other country. Never ever again.

I am going to bring our jobs back to Ohio and Pennsylvania, and New York, and Michigan, and all of America – and I am not going to let companies move to other countries, firing their employees along the way, without consequence. Not going to happen anymore.

My opponent, on the other hand, has supported virtually every trade agreement that has been destroying our middle class. She supported NAFTA, and she supported China's entrance into the World Trade Organization – another one of her husband's colossal mistakes and disasters.

She supported the job-killing trade deal with South Korea. She supported the Trans-Pacific Partnership. Which will not only destroy our manufacturers, but will make America subject to the rulings of foreign governments. And it's not going to happen.

I pledge to never sign any trade agreement that hurts our workers or that diminishes our freedom or independence. We will never sign bad trade deals. America First again. America First.

Instead, I will make individual deals with individual countries. No longer will we enter into these massive *transactions*, with many countries, that are thousands of pages long – and which no one from our country even reads or understands.
We are going to enforce all trade violations, against any country that cheats.

This includes stopping China's outrageous theft of intellectual property, along with their illegal product dumping, and their devastating currency manipulation. They are the greatest that ever came about. They are the greatest currency manipulators ever.

Our horrible trade agreements with China and many others will be totally renegotiated. That includes renegotiating NAFTA to get a much better deal for America – and we'll walk away if we don't get that kind of a deal.

Our country is going to start building and making things again.

Next comes the reform of our tax laws, regulations and energy rules. While Hillary Clinton plans a massive, and I mean massive, tax increase, I have proposed the largest tax reduction of any candidate who has run for the president this year – Democrat or Republican.

Middle-income Americans and businesses will experience profound relief, and taxes will be greatly simplified for everyone. I mean everyone.

America is one of the highest-taxed nations in the world.

Reducing taxes will cause new companies and new jobs to come roaring back into our country. Believe me, it'll happen and it'll happen fast.

Then we are going to deal with the issue of regulation, one of the greatest job-killers of them all. Excessive regulation is costing our country as much as $2 trillion a year, and we will end it *very, very quickly.*

We are going to lift the restrictions on the production of American energy.

This will produce more than $20 trillion in job-creating economic activity over the next four decades. My opponent, on the other hand, wants to put the great miners and the great steelworkers of our country out of work and out of business – that will never happen with Donald J Trump as president. Our steelworkers and our miners are going back to work again.

With these new economic policies, trillions and trillions of dollars will start flowing into our country. This new wealth will improve the quality of life for all Americans – We will build the roads, highways, bridges, tunnels, airports, and the railways of tomorrow. This, in turn, will create millions of more jobs. We will rescue kids from failing schools by helping their parents send them to a safe school of their choice.

My opponent would rather protect bureaucrats than serve American children. And that's what she's doing. And that's what's she's done. We will repeal and replace disastrous Obamacare.

You will be able to choose your own doctor again.

And we will fix TSA at the airports! Which is a total disaster.

We're going to work with all of our students who are drowning in debt to take the pressure off these young people just starting out in their adult lives. Tremendous problem.

We will completely rebuild our depleted military, and the countries that we protect, at a massive cost to us, will be asked to pay their fair share.

We will take care of our great Veterans like they have never been taken care of before.

My just released 10 point plan has received tremendous veteran support. We will guarantee those who serve this country will be able to visit the doctor or hospital of their choice without waiting five days on a line and dying.

My opponent dismissed the VA scandal. One more sign of how out of touch she really is. We are going to ask every Department Head in government to provide a list of wasteful spending projects that we can eliminate in my first 100 days.

The politicians have talked about this for years, but I'm going to do it.

We are going to appoint justices of the United States Supreme Court who will uphold our laws and our Constitution.

The replacement of our beloved Justice Scalia will be a person of similar views and principles and judicial philosophies. Very important. This will be one of the most important issues decided by this election. My opponent wants to essentially abolish the 2nd amendment.

I, on the other hand, received the early and strong endorsement of the National Rifle Association and will protect the right of all Americans to keep their families safe.

At this moment, I would like to thank the evangelical and religious community because I'll tell you what. Because the support they've given me, and I'm not sure I totally deserve it, has been so amazing. And has had such a big reason for me being here tonight. True. So true.

They have so much to contribute to our politics, yet our laws prevent you from speaking your minds from your own pulpits. An amendment, pushed by Lyndon Johnson, many years ago, threatens religious institutions with a loss of their tax-exempt status if they openly advocate their political views. Their voice has been taken away.

I am going to work very hard to repeal that language and *to* protect free speech for all Americans.
We can accomplish these great things, and so much more – all we need to do is start believing in ourselves and in our country again. Start believing. It is time to show the whole world that America Is Back – bigger, and better and stronger than ever before.

In this journey, I'm so lucky to have at my side my wife Melania and my wonderful children, Don, Ivanka, Eric, Tiffany, and Barron: you will always be my greatest source of pride and joy. And by the way, Melania and Ivanka, did they do a job.

[There's also a bit more of the personal in this speech. Trump not only talks about his children, as he often does, but also his parents and siblings. This week we've seen an effort to humanize a man who is known for being bold and confrontational, and that continues here. — Sarah McCammon]

My Dad, Fred Trump, was the smartest and hardest working man I ever knew. I wonder sometimes what he'd say if he were here to see this, and to see me, tonight.

It's because of him that I learned, from my youngest age, to respect the dignity of work and the dignity of working people.

He was a guy most comfortable in the company of bricklayers, and carpenters, and electricians and I have a lot of that in me also. I love those people.

Then there's my mother, Mary. She was strong, but also warm and fair-minded. She was a truly great mother. She was also one of the most honest and charitable people I have ever known, and a great great judge of character. She could pick 'em out from anywhere.

To my sisters Mary Anne and Elizabeth, my brother Robert and my late brother Fred, I will always give you my love you are most special to me.

I have had a truly great life in business. But now, my sole and exclusive mission is to go to work for our country – to go to work for you. It's time to deliver a victory for the American people. We don't win anymore, but we are going to start winning again.

But to do that, we must break free from the petty politics of the past. America is a nation of believers, dreamers, and strivers that is being led by a group of censors, critics, and cynics.

Remember: all of the people telling you you can't have the country you want, are the same people telling you that wouldn't stand, I mean they said Trump doesn't have a chance of being here tonight. Not a chance. The same people. Oh we love defeating those people. Don't we? Don't we? Love it. Love it. Love it.

No longer can we rely on those same people in the media media, and politics, who will say anything to keep a rigged system in place.

Instead, we must choose to Believe In America. History is watching us now. We don't have much time, but history is watching. It's waiting to see if we will rise to the occasion, and if we will show the whole world that America is still free and independent and strong.

I am asking for your support tonight so I can be your champion in the White House. And I will be your champion.

My opponent asks her supporters to recite a three-word loyalty pledge. It reads: "I'm With Her". I choose to recite a different pledge.
My pledge reads: "I'M WITH YOU – THE AMERICAN PEOPLE."

I am your voice. So to every parent who dreams for their child, and every child who dreams for their future, I say these words to you tonight: I am With You, and I will fight for you, and I will win for you.

To all Americans tonight, in all of our cities and in all of our towns, I make this promise: We Will Make America Strong Again. We Will Make America Proud Again. We Will Make America Safe Again. And We Will Make America Great Again.

God bless you, and goodnight. I love you.

SENATOR BERNIE SANDERS

Bernie Sander's Presidential Campaign Announcement Speech on May 26,
2015

"Thank you all very much for being here and for all the support that
you have given me over the years: as the mayor of this great city, as
Vermont's only congressman and now as a U.S. senator. Thanks also
to my longtime friends and fellow Vermonters Bill McKibben,
Brenda Torpey, Donna Bailey, Mike O'Day and Ben and Jerry for
all that you do – and for your very generous remarks. Thanks also to
Jenny Nelson for moderating this event and for your leadership in
Vermont agriculture.

I also want to thank my family: My wife Jane, my brother Larry, my
children Levi, Heather, Carina and Dave for their love and support,
and my seven beautiful grandchildren – Sonny, Cole, Ryleigh,
Grayson, Ella, Tess and Dylan who provide so much joy in my life.

Today, here in our small state – a state that has led the nation in so
many ways – I am proud to announce my candidacy for President of
the United States of America.

Today, with your support and the support of millions of people
throughout this country, we begin a political revolution to transform
our country economically, politically, socially and environmentally.

Today, we stand here and say loudly and clearly that; "Enough is
enough. This great nation and its government belong to all of the
people, and not to a handful of billionaires, their Super-PACs and
their lobbyists."

Brothers and sisters: Now is not the time for thinking small. Now is
not the time for the same old – same old establishment politics and
stale inside-the-beltway ideas.

Now is the time for millions of working families to come together, to revitalize American democracy, to end the collapse of the American middle class and to make certain that our children and grandchildren are able to enjoy a quality of life that brings them health, prosperity, security and joy – and that once again makes the United States the leader in the world in the fight for economic and social justice, for environmental sanity and for a world of peace.

My fellow Americans: This country faces more serious problems today than at any time since the Great Depression and, if you include the planetary crisis of climate change, it may well be that the challenges we face now are direr than any time in our modern history.

Here is my promise to you for this campaign. Not only will I fight to protect the working families of this country, but we're going to build a movement of millions of Americans who are prepared to stand up and fight back. We're going to take this campaign directly to the people – in town meetings, door to door conversations, on street corners and in social media – and that's BernieSanders.com by the way. This week we will be in New Hampshire, Iowa and Minnesota – and that's just the start of a vigorous grassroots campaign.

Let's be clear. This campaign is not about Bernie Sanders. It is not about Hillary Clinton. It is not about Jeb Bush or anyone else. This campaign is about the needs of the American people, and the ideas and proposals that effectively address those needs. As someone who has never run a negative political ad in his life, my campaign will be driven by issues and serious debate; not political gossip, not reckless personal attacks or character assassination. This is what I believe the American people want and deserve. I hope other candidates agree, and I hope the media allows that to happen. Politics in a democratic society should not be treated like a baseball game, a game show or a soap opera. The times are too serious for that.

Let me take a minute to touch on some of the issues that I will be
focusing on in the coming months, and then give you an outline of
an Agenda for America which will, in fact, deal with these problems
and lead us to a better future.

Income and Wealth Inequality: Today, we live in the wealthiest
nation in the history of the world but that reality means very little for
most of us because almost all of that wealth is owned and controlled
by a tiny handful of individuals. In America we now have more
income and wealth inequality than any other major country on earth,
and the gap between the very rich and everyone is wider than at any
time since the 1920s. The issue of wealth and income inequality is
the great moral issue of our time, it is the great economic issue of
our time and it is the great political issue of our time. And we will
address it.

Let me be very clear. There is something profoundly wrong when
the top one-tenth of 1 percent owns almost as much wealth as the
bottom 90 percent, and when 99 percent of all new income goes to
the top 1 percent. There is something profoundly wrong when, in
recent years, we have seen a proliferation of millionaires and
billionaires at the same time as millions of Americans work longer
hours for lower wages and we have the highest rate of childhood
poverty of any major country on earth. There is something
profoundly wrong when one family owns more wealth than the
bottom 130 million Americans. This grotesque level of inequality is
immoral. It is bad economics. It is unsustainable. This type of rigged
economy is not what America is supposed to be about. This has got
to change and, as your president, together we will change it.

Economics: But it is not just income and wealth inequality. It is the
tragic reality that for the last 40 years the great middle class of our
country – once the envy of the world – has been disappearing.
Despite exploding technology and increased worker productivity,
median family income is almost $5,000 less than it was in 1999. In
Vermont and throughout this country it is not uncommon for people
to be working two or three jobs just to cobble together enough
income to survive on and some health care benefits.

The truth is that real unemployment is not the 5.4 percent you read in newspapers. It is close to 11 percent if you include those workers who have given up looking for jobs or who are working part time when they want to work full time. Youth unemployment is over 17 percent and African-American youth unemployment is much higher than that. Today, shamefully, we have 45 million people living in poverty, many of whom are working at low-wage jobs. These are the people who struggle every day to find the money to feed their kids, to pay their electric bills and to put gas in the car to get to work. This campaign is about those people and our struggling middle class. It is about creating an economy that works for all, and not just the one percent.

Citizens United: My fellow Americans: Let me be as blunt as I can and tell you what you already know. As a result of the disastrous Supreme Court decision on Citizens United, the American political system has been totally corrupted, and the foundations of American democracy are being undermined. What the Supreme Court essentially said was that it was not good enough for the billionaire class to own much of our economy. They could now own the U.S. government as well. And that is precisely what they are trying to do.

American democracy is not about billionaires being able to buy candidates and elections. It is not about the Koch brothers, Sheldon Adelson and other incredibly wealthy individuals spending billions of dollars to elect candidates who will make the rich richer and everyone else poorer. According to media reports the Koch brothers alone, one family, will spend more money in this election cycle than either the Democratic or Republican parties. This is not democracy. This is oligarchy. In Vermont and at our town meetings we know what American democracy is supposed to be about. It is one person, one vote – with every citizen having an equal say – and no voter suppression. And that's the kind of American political system we have to fight for and will fight for in this campaign.

Climate Change: When we talk about our responsibilities as human beings and as parents, there is nothing more important than leaving this country and the entire planet in a way that is habitable for our kids and grandchildren. The debate is over. The scientific community has spoken in a virtually unanimous voice. Climate change is real. It is caused by human activity and it is already causing devastating problems in the United States and around the world.

The scientists are telling us that if we do not boldly transform our energy system away from fossil fuels and into energy efficiency and sustainable energies, this planet could be five to ten degrees Fahrenheit warmer by the end of this century. This is catastrophic. It will mean more drought, more famine, more rising sea level, more floods, more ocean acidification, more extreme weather disturbances, more disease and more human suffering. We must not, we cannot, and we will not allow that to happen.

It is no secret that there is massive discontent with politics in America today. In the mid-term election in November, 63 percent of Americans did not vote, including 80 percent of young people. Poll after poll tells us that our citizens no longer have confidence in our political institutions and, given the power of Big Money in the political process, they have serious doubts about how much their vote actually matters and whether politicians have any clue as to what is going on in their lives.

Combatting this political alienation, this cynicism and this legitimate anger will not be easy. That's for sure. But that is exactly what, together, we have to do if we are going to turn this country around – and that is what this campaign is all about.

And to bring people together we need a simple and straight-forward progressive agenda which speaks to the needs of our people, and which provides us with a vision of a very different America. And what is that agenda?

Jobs, Jobs, Jobs: It begins with jobs. If we are truly serious about reversing the decline of the middle class we need a major federal jobs program which puts millions of Americans back to work at decent paying jobs. At a time when our roads, bridges, water systems, rail and airports are decaying, the most effective way to rapidly create meaningful jobs is to rebuild our crumbling infrastructure. That's why I've introduced legislation which would invest $1 trillion over 5 years to modernize our country's physical infrastructure. This legislation would create and maintain at least 13 million good-paying jobs, while making our country more productive, efficient and safe. And I promise you as president I will lead that legislation into law.

I will also continue to oppose our current trade policies. For decades, presidents from both parties have supported trade agreements which have cost us millions of decent paying jobs as corporate America shuts down plants here and moves to low-wage countries. As president, my trade policies will break that cycle of agreements which enrich at the expense of the working people of this country.

Raising Wages: Let us be honest and acknowledge that millions of Americans are now working for totally inadequate wages. The current federal minimum wage of $7.25 an hour is a starvation wage and must be raised. The minimum wage must become a living wage – which means raising it to $15 an hour over the next few years – which is exactly what Los Angeles recently did – and I applaud them for doing that. Our goal as a nation must be to ensure that no full-time worker lives in poverty. Further, we must establish pay equity for women workers. It's unconscionable that women earn 78 cents on the dollar compared to men who perform the same work. We must also end the scandal in which millions of American employees, often earning less than $30,000 a year, work 50 or 60 hours a week – and earn no overtime. And we need paid sick leave and guaranteed vacation time for all.

Addressing Wealth and Income Inequality: This campaign is going to send a message to the billionaire class. And that is: you can't have it all. You can't get huge tax breaks while children in this country go hungry. You can't continue sending our jobs to China while millions are looking for work. You can't hide your profits in the Cayman Islands and other tax havens, while there are massive unmet needs on every corner of this nation. Your greed has got to end. You cannot take advantage of all the benefits of America, if you refuse to accept your responsibilities.

That is why we need a tax system which is fair and progressive, which makes wealthy individuals and profitable corporations begin to pay their fair share of taxes.

Reforming Wall Street: It is time to break up the largest financial institutions in the country. Wall Street cannot continue to be an island unto itself, gambling trillions in risky financial instruments while expecting the public to bail it out. If a bank is too big to fail it is too big to exist. We need a banking system which is part of the job creating productive economy, not a handful of huge banks on Wall Street which engage in reckless and illegal activities.

Campaign Finance Reform: If we are serious about creating jobs, about climate change and the needs of our children and the elderly, we must be deadly serious about campaign finance reform and the need for a constitutional amendment to overturn Citizens United. I have said it before and I'll say it again. I will not nominate any justice to the Supreme Court who has not made it clear that he or she will move to overturn that disastrous decision which is undermining our democracy. Long term, we need to go further and establish public funding of elections.

Reversing Climate Change: The United States must lead the world in reversing climate change. We can do that if we transform our energy system away from fossil fuels, toward energy efficiency and such sustainable energies such as wind, solar, geo-thermal and bio-mass. Millions of homes and buildings need to be weatherized, our transportation system needs to be energy efficient, and we need a tax on carbon to accelerate the transition away from fossil fuel.

Health Care for All: The United States remains the only major country on earth that does not guarantee health care for all as a right. Despite the modest gains of the Affordable Care Act, 35 million Americans continue to lack health insurance and many more are under-insured. Yet, we continue paying far more per capita for health care than any other nation. The United States must join the rest of the industrialized world and guarantee health care to all as a right by moving toward a Medicare-for-All single-payer system.

Protecting Our Most Vulnerable: At a time when millions of Americans are struggling to keep their heads above water economically, at a time when senior poverty is increasing, at a time when millions of kids are living in dire poverty, my Republican colleagues, as part of their recently-passed budget, are trying to make a terrible situation even worse. If you can believe it, the Republican budget throws 27 million Americans off health insurance, makes drastic cuts in Medicare, throws millions of low-income Americans, including pregnant women off of nutrition programs, and makes it harder for working-class families to afford college or put their kids in the Head Start program. And then, to add insult to injury, they provide huge tax breaks for the very wealthiest families in this country while they raise taxes on working families.

Well, let me tell my Republican colleagues that I respectfully disagree with their approach. Instead of cutting Social Security, we're going to expand Social Security benefits. Instead of cutting Head Start and child care, we are going to move to a universal pre-K system for all the children of this country. As Franklin Delano Roosevelt reminded us, a nation's greatness is judged not by what it provides to the most well-off, but how it treats the people most in need. And that's the kind of nation we must become.

College for All: And when we talk about education, let me be very clear. In a highly competitive global economy, we need the best educated workforce we can create. It is insane and counter-productive to the best interests of our country, that hundreds of thousands of bright young people cannot afford to go to college, and that millions of others leave school with a mountain of debt that burdens them for decades. That must end. That is why, as president, I will fight to make tuition in public colleges and universities free, as well as substantially lower interest rates on student loans.

War and Peace: As everybody knows, we live in a difficult and dangerous world, and there are people out there who want to do us harm. As president, I will defend this nation – but I will do it responsibly. As a member of Congress I voted against the war in Iraq, and that was the right vote. I am vigorously opposed to an endless war in the Middle East – a war which is unwise and unnecessary. We must be vigorous in combatting terrorism and defeating ISIS, but we should not have to bear that burden alone. We must be part of an international coalition, led by Muslim nations, that can not only defeat ISIS but begin the process of creating conditions for a lasting peace.

As some of you know, I was born in a far-away land called Brooklyn, New York. My father came to this country from Poland without a penny in his pocket and without much of an education. My mother graduated high school in New York City. My father worked for almost his entire life as a paint salesman and we were solidly lower-middle class. My parents, brother and I lived in a small rent-controlled apartment. My mother's dream was to move out of that small apartment into a home of our own. She died young and her dream was never fulfilled. As a kid I learned, in many, many ways, what lack of money means to a family. That's a lesson I have never forgotten.

I have seen the promise of America in my own life. My parents would have never dreamed that their son would be a U.S. Senator, let alone run for president. But for too many of our fellow Americans, the dream of progress and opportunity is being denied by the grind of an economy that funnels all the wealth to the top.

And to those who say we cannot restore the dream, I say just look where we are standing. This beautiful place was once an unsightly rail yard that served no public purpose and was an eyesore. As mayor, I worked with the people of Burlington to help turn this waterfront into the beautiful people-oriented public space it is today. We took the fight to the courts, to the legislature and to the people. And we won.

The lesson to be learned is that when people stand together, and are prepared to fight back, there is nothing that can't be accomplished.

We can live in a country:

- Where every person has health care as a right, not a privilege;
- Where every parent can have quality and affordable childcare and where all of our qualified young people, regardless of income, can go to college;
- Where every senior can live in dignity and security, and not be forced to choose between their medicine or their food;

- Where every veteran who defends this nation gets the quality health care and benefits they have earned and receives the respect they deserve;
- Where every person, no matter their race, their religion, their disability or their sexual orientation realizes the full promise of equality that is our birthright as Americans.

That is the nation we can build together, and I ask you to join me in this campaign to build a future that works for all of us, and not just the few on top.

Thank you, and on this beautiful day on the shore of Lake Champlain, I welcome you aboard."

My Summary Remarks on the Speeches

One could read and analyze any speech that any candidate gave and get an idea of not only their personality type but also could discern the types of techniques and gambits they were employing to sell themselves to the voters. In spite of the professional speech writers' heavy influence who politicians employ, over the course of a campaign there is a consistency of sorts. So, in this case, I chose just one speech from each candidate as it was a significant one for each.

Chapter 12: RESOURCES

Speech Techniques Checklist: If you would like a handy list of the selling techniques listed in this book, go to www.CodeBlueInTheWhiteHouse.com and sign up to have it emailed to you. You can use this checklist when you are listening to or reading a candidate's speech to more clearly classify the methods they are (1) using to sell to you and (2) trying to get your financial and voting support.

Recommended and Referenced Books

Thom Hartmann: **Cracking the Code: How to Win Hearts, Change Minds, and Restore America's Original Vision (2007)** (Perceptive analysis of presidential speeches related to Neurolinguistic programming and the survival brain.)

Clint Arthur: **21 Performance Secrets of Donald Trump (2016)**

Clint Arthur: **President's Code: Common Traits of Uncommon Leaders (2012)**

Chris Carey: **Getting to Know You: How You Can Solve Your "People Puzzles" and Increase Success in All Your Personal and Professional Relationships (2002)** (About DISC)

Anthony Robbins: **Unlimited Power: The New Science of Personal Achievement (2008)** (In depth discussion of Neurolinguistic Programming)

Republican and Democratic Presidential Candidates' Website descriptions

I find it fascinating to read the descriptions of the websites of the candidates. These, on the face of them, give insight into the persona of the candidates and are suggestive as to their personality type.

Donald Trump - Official Site

https://www.donaldjtrump.com

Donald J. Trump is the very definition of the American success story, continually setting the standards of excellence in business, real estate and entertainment. Show ...

Bernie Sanders for President | Contribute to Bernie Sanders

https://berniesanders.com

The official campaign website for the presidential campaign of United States Senator Bernie Sanders.

Hillary Clinton - Official Site

https://www.hillaryclinton.com

Official campaign site of Hillary for America. Hillary Clinton wants to be a champion for everyday Americans - so she's a candidate for president in 2016.

BOOKS by Hillary Clinton, Bernie Sanders, and Donald Trump,

The titles of the books that each candidate has authored, co-authored, or had ghost-written also adds to the tapestry of who they are and what they intend to portray. It tells about their values and policies. For example, the most obvious ones to me are by and for Donald Trump. A vast majority have his name in the title and not just as author. This is very WIFM and ACTION type.

Hillary Clinton: *It Takes a Village: And Other Lessons Children Teach Us. Dear Socks, Dear Buddy: Kids' Letters to the First Pets* (1998) *An Invitation to the White House: At Home with History* (2000), autobiography *Living History,* a second memoir, *Hard Choices,* which focused on her time as Secretary of State.

Bernie Sanders: *Outsider in the White House* coauthored Bernie Sanders and John Nichols

Donald Trump: ***Trump: The Art of the Deal* (1987), co-written with Tony Schwartz,** *Surviving at the Top* **(1990),** *The Art of Survival* (1991), *The Art of the Comeback* (1997), co-written with Kate Bohner, *The America We Deserve* (2000), with Dave Shiflett, According to Wikipedia, the following are books authored by the current top runners. Just looking at the titles tells us a lot about the personality type and values of the author. Some are other oriented, some are "me" oriented, some talk about policy, some talk about the big picture. *How to Get Rich* (2004), *The Way to the Top: The Best Business Advice I Ever Received* (2004), *Trump: Think Like a Billionaire: Everything You Need to Know About Success, Real Estate, and Life* (2004),

Trump: The Best Golf Advice I Ever Received (2005), *Why We
Want You to be Rich: Two Men – One Message* (2006), co-written
with Robert Kiyosaki, *Think Big and Kick Ass in Business and
Life* (2007), co-written with Bill Zanker, *Trump: The Best Real
Estate Advice I Ever Received: 100 Top Experts Share Their
Strategies* (2007), *Trump 101: The Way to Success* (2007), *Trump
Never Give Up: How I Turned My Biggest Challenges into Success*
(2008), *Think Like a Champion: An Informal Education in Business
and Life* (2009),*Midas Touch: Why Some Entrepreneurs Get Rich –
and Why Most Don't* (2011), co-written with Robert T.
Kiyosaki, *Time to Get Tough: Making America No. 1 Again*
(2011), *Crippled America: How to Make America Great Again*
(2015),

Heights of some other Politicians and Famous People

Continuing on the (tenuous) thought thread established
earlier in Chapters 2 and 10, I am including the heights of
some other well-known people to provide some additional
fodder for chewing on. Consider if it makes any difference
when thinking about the effects of a person's body size has on
perception, power and influence. No relationship between
any of the people on this list is implied – they are just listed by
how tall they are reported to be on the internet.

Osama Ben Lauden	6' 5"	1.95 m
Franklin D. Roosevelt	6' 2"	1.88 m
Arnold Schwarzenegger	6' 1.5"	1.87 m
Saddam Hussein	6' 1"	1.86 m
Eleanor Roosevelt	6' 0"	1.84 m

Sting	6' 0"	1.83 m
Sigourney Weaver	5' 11"	1.80 m
Brad Pitt	5' 11"	1.80 m
Taylor Swift	5' 9.5"	1.77 m
Rihanna	5' 8"	1.73 m
Adolf Hitler	5' 8"	1.73 m
Joseph Stalin	5' 8"	1.73 m
Adolf Hitler	5' 8"	1.73 m
John McCain	5' 7"	1.70 m
Beyoncé	5' 7"	1.69 m
Bono	5' 6"	1.68 m
Winston Churchill	5' 6"	1.67 m
Hillary Rodham Clinton	5' 5.5"	1.66 m
Sarah Palin	5' 5.5"	1.65 m

Author Biography

Thousands of patients have benefited by the evaluation and
treatments using acupuncture, herbs, naturopathic supplements,
shiatsu massage, NRCT, weight loss programs, detoxification

programs, and other modalities with Dr. Jay Sordean. In order to
promote his mission to prevent 1 million cases of dementia and
Alzheimer's, best-selling author and clinician Dr. Jay has appeared
on televisions stations around the U.S., including ABC, CBS, NBC,
FOX, and CW. Dr. Jay has lectured to diverse audiences on keys to
preserving their brains and memory. He is available for TV
appearances and as a speaker on B.A.N.K.™ Code, brain health,
improving memory, and company wellness programs that address
these issues. His other books also discuss how your brain works, a
key factor in this book—how politicians get you to vote for them.

Training and Credentials

Dr. John R. "Dr. Jay" Sordean uses his medical experience—as a licensed acupuncturist (L.Ac.), Oriental Medical Doctor (O.M.D.), Certified Traditional Naturopath (C.T.N.), Qualified Medical Evaluator (Q.M.E.), homeopath, and herbalist—to promote an understanding of good health for culturally diverse communities.

Dr. Sordean has treated an extensive range of health issues, and specializes in the brain, pediatrics, immunology, orthopedic and neurological acupuncture, and herbology. He has been certified as a Diplomate of Acupuncture by the National Certification Commission for Acupuncture and Oriental Medicine and the National Board of Acupuncture Orthopedics.

In 2005, he achieved Medical Provider certification in the First Line Therapy program, which leads patients to optimal health and body composition through balanced eating, exercise, stress reduction, appropriate testing (toxicity, body mass), and nutritional supplements.

In 2009, Dr. Sordean completed training in the Neurologic Relief Center Technique to treat fibromyalgia, chronic pain, migraine headaches, Parkinson's, TMJ, MS, and rheumatoid arthritis. Less than one percent of California and national licensed acupuncturists have achieved this level of advanced training.

Focus on Oriental Medicine

Fluent in Japanese, Dr. Sordean offers his patients techniques and treatments rare among Western doctors. He began his study of Oriental Medicine with Tai Qi Chuan and Shiatsu and immersed himself in Japanese culture while at Earlham College, a Quaker school. Dr.Sordean's formal training in acupuncture and herbology began on a 1973 trip to Japan, and continued in China (Taiwan, Hong Kong); his homeopathic training included clinical study in Calcutta, India. He later earned Practitioner of Classical Homeopathy status from the Dynamis School of Advanced Homeopathic Studies, in Canada.

Sales and Relationship Training Programs

Sales (and relationships) are not simply a matter of getting more "No's" so you can get to the "Yes's" as many sales trainers will tell you. Sales are a people "game." Relationships are a people "game." And relationships, as discussed in this book, are also and issue of sales. By means of the secret, science, and system of B.A.N.K. ™ Code communication can improve, leading to up to a 300% increase in Yes's. And "yes's" are what a happy life and business is all about. Dr. Jay Sordean is available as a speaker and trainer for your company and organization related to the quick and effective application of personality typing to effect positive change and better results in this people-oriented world we live in.

Public Service

Dr. Sordean has been active in Northern California community affairs since his move to Berkeley over 30 years ago. He has been a member of the Berkeley, Emeryville, Albany and Richmond chambers of commerce and has given educational talks to Rotary, Kiwanis, hospitals, police, senior centers, and other service groups. He served on the Board of the California Acupuncture Association. He serves on the board of the Berkeley Sakai Association (a sister-city non-profit), H.A.A.R.T., and the People's Life Fund.

Patient and Customer Satisfaction

Dr. Sordean's clients cite his sensitivity and expertise in resolving their individual needs— treatment for acute pain, chronic disease, work or personal injury—or promoting lifelong good health and disease prevention. Patients also value his open communication with their primary- care physicians and his advocacy of a holistic and preventative approach to health. See http:// www.theredwoodclinic.com for testimonials and other conditions we treat effectively. Patients and customers also love working with the B.A.N.K. ™ CODE system to better understand themselves, their family members, dating, and work situations so as to succeed in their goals and purposes in life.

Information on B.A.N.K.™ CODE

Various personality assessment tools exist in the market, but how many have been statistically validated? B.A.N.K.™ Code is the only one I know of. On top of that, it has been tested and proven to work in the field for more than 15 years.

Prior to becoming a Certified and Licensed Trainer with BANKCODE, I saw through my personal experience how helpful the use of this system is for improving communication with clients, patients, sales professionals, and in my family – however imperfectly I might implement it.

Having done a study of the clinic's patient population's B.A.N.K.™ code distribution, I realized that none of the patient's had the BLUEPRINT as their primary code. This deficiency was curious and unexpected. Knowing this enabled me to improve my communication skills to connect with the BLUEPRINT individual as a patient. Not knowing this had caused the clinic to potentially have lost at least 25% of eligible patients.

How can I explain this lack of balance? Perhaps it has to do with the fact that BLUEPRINT is in the last place in my personal B.A.N.K.™ Code line-up (KNAB and KANB with N and A equal in strength). Not that I don't value being on time and following rules! We are sticklers about that at the clinic in order to respect peoples' time commitments elsewhere. So things like being on time and early, following processes, and reliability are key to having a smooth running operation and are important to me.

With respect to being on time, in my personal life I also struggle with patience and forgiveness when someone else "blows off" a scheduled event I was looking forward to. I also get miffed if I arrive quite late to a party or gathering because I am going with other people and they are just not getting it together fast enough. So in those respects my BLUEPRINT comes out pretty strong.

Another possible reason for the relative lack of first position BLUEPRINT patients (we now have a few) is that acupuncture and natural medicine are not traditional. They are considered by many in the U.S. and elsewhere as being "fringe" still. Even though they have been used and effective for thousands of years! The establishment medical system in the U.S. has taken centuries to accept other forms of medicine and there has been a sustained attack on "non-traditional" (but really more traditional) approaches to health and healing until the last 20 or so years. In California the attitude of Medical Doctors has changed so as to have a certain acceptance and support of acupuncture in spite of it being licensed since the mid-70s.

In spite of this, following tradition is one of the hallmarks of the
BLUEPRINT and mainstream medicine is what they believe in
more-so at their core. Thus, while the acupuncture and natural
medicine I practice are reliable and safe, and I have a long track
record of clinical success – backed by my decades and my
predecessors' thousands of years of experience -- some people think
that (natural medicines) are just too outside the box to consider.

The bottom line is this. In spite of all the analysis of the results of the
clinical surveys, by my doing a big picture overview of the practice I
revealed some B.A.N.K.™ Code-related areas that needed to be
addressed. So I proceeded to integrate and apply the secrets,
science and systems of the B.A.N.K.™ Method into the clinical
practice.

I suggest that every company contact me to do the same time
of analysis of their own company customer database and
employee line-up to see where personality-type deficiencies
might be hiding and sabotaging greater success. At the same
time, I believe that this system is very applicable to
understanding the political landscape and thus I wrote this
book to integrate this into the big picture of political acumen.

Thus, coming from a place where the practical applications of B.A.N.K.™ Code made a difference in real life, I decided to become a Certified and Licensed Trainer with BANKCODE. I thus am able and excited to share the secrets, science and system of B.A.N.K.™ Code with the world, all with the intention of making the world better, one person (or one company) at a time.

Further information can be obtained by going to the following links:

http://www.Four-cards.com

http://www.BankCode.com/drjay

http://www.BankCode.com/drjay/whitepaper

NOTES: